P9-DBT-373

THE
FOURTH GOSPEL

A HISTORY OF THE TEXTUAL TRADITION
OF THE ORIGINAL GREEK GOSPEL

by

Victor Salmon

translated by

Matthew J. O'Connell

THE LITURGICAL PRESS
Collegeville   Minnesota

For permission to reproduce the illustrations given in this work, the author wishes to express his gratitude to the Bodmer Library, Geneva; the Albertine Library, Brussels; the National Library, Paris; the Vatican Library, Rome; the British Museum, London; the Bodleian Library, Oxford; the Library of the University of Cambridge; the John Rylands Library, Manchester.

THE FOURTH GOSPEL — A HISTORY OF THE TEXTUAL TRADITION OF THE ORIGINAL GREEK GOSPEL is the authorized English version of *Histoire de la tradition textuelle de l'original Grec du quatrieme evangile* published by Letouzey et Ané, 87 Boulevard Raspail, Paris 6, France.

Copyright 1976 *by* The Order of St. Benedict, Inc., Collegeville, Minnesota. Printed in the U.S.A.

ISBN 0-8146-0926-0

Contents

The
Greek of the New Testament

We modern Christians read the New Testament, originally written in Greek, in a variety of translations. Each of these has its merits: accuracy, or literalness, or proximity to spoken English, or suitableness for reading aloud, and so forth. A given translation may even have several of these merits at once.

Does this mean that these translations are definitive for English-language readers? Not at all. Even the best translation into a living language becomes outdated as the language develops. More to the point, it is impossible to render perfectly into the languages currently in use a language as full of nuances as the Greek of two millennia ago.

This claim can be easily tested. Simply take the same chapter from each of several translations, and you will find different words and expressions used to translate the same original text. Since it is impossible to convey every nuance of thought or feeling, each translator has to make a choice, and the choice is always, to some extent, a betrayal.

There is need, then, of remaining in constant contact with the original Greek text. Fidelity to the latter must be the aim in every age as new translators seek a more accurate transposition of the original into contemporary languages.

How did it happen that the New Testament was written entirely in Greek?

After Alexander had conquered the Middle East, three centuries before Christ, Greek became the international language of the Mediterranean basin. It held a position similar to that of English today, insofar as the latter has become the commercial language of the modern world and the language used by all the shipping companies and airlines.

Even at Rome, Greek was the language used during their school years by Caesar and by Cicero who was trained in the oratorical art by Molon of Rhodes. The circle of Scipio Aemilianus prided itself on speaking Greek and considered Latin a language fit only for soldiers and lawyers.

Jesus spoke Aramaic to his disciples and preached in that language as well, but it is quite possible that he answered the centurion in Greek, since the population of Galilee included a large number of foreigners.

When we try to estimate the influence exercised by the language of the Greek conqueror, we must bear in mind that the Sadducees, and especially the priests among them, were collaborators with the Romans.

Pilate, as a Roman official, must have known Greek, and nothing indicates that he did not use this international language which foreigners and even the Jews of the Diaspora would know.

We must rid ourselves of the idea that the disciples of Jesus were all fishermen and illiterate peasants. John and James were sons of a man who owned fishing boats, and John was known to the high priest. Matthew was a tax collector and could not have dealt with foreigners unless he had some knowledge of the international language.

Greek was the language in which Christianity was given to the world, and would for four centuries be the language of Christian writers throughout the entire Eastern world. For more than a century it would be the language of liturgy, even at Rome.

The Greek in question was, of course, no longer the language of Demosthenes, any more than our present-day English is the language of Shakespeare. Pronunciation, grammar, and syntax had all undergone changes. Yet the language was still Greek: a thing of beauty to the ear; simpler than the Greek of Plato, but capable of untranslatable subtleties and of a flexibility that made it unique among the Indo-European languages (consider, for example, how St. Paul was able to use it).

In writing their books which shaped the western world, the evangelists used this *Koine* Greek, the second language which all travellers in the Mediterranean world learned.

The new body of religious thought that emerged during the first century of our era had its roots in the Old Testament. But the Old Testament texts quoted in the Gospels were not translated directly from Hebrew or Aramaic; they were taken from the Septuagint or Greek translation of the Old Testament. Many Jews, particularly in the Diaspora, had forgotten their ancestral language and used a Greek translation done in the Jewish colony at Alexandria; according to legend, the translation had been made by seventy, or more accurately seventy-two, Hebrew scholars around 200 B.C. (whence the name "Septuagint" or "Seventy"). The Greek of this translation abounded in semitisms.

The task of the New Testament writers, however, was not to emphasize the Jewish origins of Christianity but to present Christianity as an independent reality. These writers wished to convey a world of events and new ideas, and to do it in a Greek that everyone in the Mediterranean area could understand. For this task they needed a new terminology. The Gospels are full of ancient words, such as "Logos" ("word"), which were as old as Homer. Many of these words were used in present-ing ideas that came into the world with the teaching of Jesus.

Evidently there is no less difficulty in finding equivalents for these words in our contemporary languages, especially if we want a clear and readable version.

The formation of the Gospels has been dealt with by countless writers. The synoptic question is without relevance to our purpose here. ("Synoptic" implies that the three Gospels of Mark, Matthew, and Luke can be set up in three columns so that the parallel passages may be read side by side.)

In order to make it easier for someone with a little knowledge of Greek to read the present book, as many as possible of the paleographic reproductions will be taken from the Gospel of John, chapter 18, verses 28-40, the account of Jesus' trial before Pilate. Plate 64 in the album provides a Greek text which the reader can use for comparison with the translations he possesses. Most English translations in recent years claim to be based on the original text.

Where do we find what may with some exaggeration be called "the original text"? In critical editions of the Greek New Testament.

The most important names and dates in the elaboration of a critical text are: Erasmus, in 1516; the polyglot New Testament of Alcalá, in 1520 ("Complutensian Polyglot"); the great edition by Tischendorf, in 1872; the Greek New Testament of Westcott and Hort, in 1881; and, finally, Nestle's edition, in 1898. A splendid critical edition of this last was published in 1967, under the direction of Kurt Aland.

But printed books have a manuscript ancestry. If we move backward through history, we find: (1) from the sixteenth to the ninth centuries, 2,754 manuscripts in minuscule letters that are often cursive (i.e., con-nected as in our modern handwriting); (2) from the eighth to the fourth centuries, manuscripts in majuscule letters that may be either capitals, such as were used in inscriptions, or uncials (rounded letters), 266 in number; (3) finally, 81 biblical papyri discovered since the beginning of the twentieth century take us back (for the fourth Gospel) to within some years of the traditional date of composition, namely, the last decade of the first century of the Christian era. We shall be following this se-quence from the other direction and in greater detail.

One final prefatory point. Why are we publishing this work of scien-tific popularization with its numerous plates? A first reason is that there are few comparable books available in English. The Introductions to the Old and New Testaments, edited by A. Robert and A. Feuillet, for all their vast length contain only four reproductions of texts and do not offer any explanation of the plates for the uninitiated. The present essay aims at making it easier for anyone who knows the Greek alphabet to come to grips with the reproductions of the texts. A further reason is that an impartial examination of the text tradition as critically established will allow any fair person to judge the historical value of the Gospels, especially the fourth. A few examples will show how far people are from making such a fair judgment.

In 1962 a beautifully printed book appeared at Moscow, written by a Mr. Cheinman; its title was *The Vatican of Our Day.* "When Catholic literature claims that Peter the Apostle was the first Pope, it does so in order to establish a direct link between the contemporary papacy and the Prince of the Apostles. But the claim is false, if for no other reason than that the Apostle Peter is no less mythical a figure than Jesus Christ himself" (p. 57).

All major libraries have Solomon Reinach's *Orpheus* on their shelves. The 1933 edition of the book is a reprint of the 1909 edition, in which the documentation dates from the nineteenth century. It is not surprising that Reinach's pages on the fourth Gospel have no historical value today, since twentieth century paleographical finds have put the problem of the antiquity of the fourth Gospel in an entirely new light.

The worthlessness of these two books is clear. One is propaganda, the other lacked access to the necessary documents.

We reach the nadir in the January 1967 issue of the periodical *Sciences et avenir.* In it, H. de Saint-Blanquart takes us on a pilgrimage to the sources of our Bible. A photograph of the Codex Vaticanus, containing the beginning of the Letter of James, carries the caption: "Greek translation; the manuscript dates from 1209." 1209 is the classification number in the Vatican Library.

What confidence can be put in such a writer? The original text of James is in Greek, and the Codex dates from about 330. It is difficult to comprehend such a contempt for historical fact in dealing with readers who have neither the time nor the specialized training required for searching out and verifying the real historical facts.

Amid the accumulation of encyclopedic knowledge that marks our culture, this essay seeks only to initiate the reader into certain historical facts: the papyri and manuscripts of the New Testament.

Contemporary exegesis of the fourth Gospel can rely on new paleographic material discovered within the past century. We shall show that this material brings us to within a few years of the time when the text of John was composed.

Our essay is not a work of exegesis. We shall, however, point out various commentaries to the reader. The abundant bibliography at the end of each chapter will enable the reader to check everything we say if he has access to a major university library.

General Bibliography

A. *General Introductions to the Study of the New Testament*
   Kenyon, Frederic George, *Our Bible and the Ancient Manuscripts*, rev. by A. W. Adams. New York: Harper, 1958.

Lagrange, Marie-Joseph, O.P., and Stanislas Lyonnet, S.J., *Critique textuelle* II: *La critique rationnelle* (Introduction à l'étude du Nouveau Testament 2). Paris: Gabalda, 1935.

Metzger, Bruce M., *The Text of the New Testament: Its Transmission, Corruption and Restoration.* New York: Oxford University Press, 1964.

Robert, André, and André Feuillet (eds.), *Introduction to the Old Testament,* tr. by Patrick W. Skehan *et al.* from the second edition of *Introduction à la Bible* 1: *Introduction Générale; Ancien Testament* (Tournai: Desclée, 1959). New York: Desclee, 1968. But the "Introduction Générale" was not included in the English translation; separate publication of it was intended.

————, *Introduction to the New Testament,* tr. by Patrick W. Skehan *et al.* from the second edition of *Introduction à la Bible* 2: *Nouveau Testament* (Tournai: Desclée, 1959). New York: Desclee, 1965.

Vaganay, Léon, *Introduction to the Textual Criticism of the New Testament,* tr. by B. V. Miller from *Initiation à la critique textuelle néotestamentaire* (Paris: Bloud, 1934). St. Louis: B. Herder, 1937.

Wikenhauser, Alfred, *New Testament Introduction,* tr. by Joseph Cunningham from *Einleitung in das Neue Testament* (Freiburg im Breisgau: Herder, 1956). New York: Herder and Herder, 1958.

B. *Greek Text of the New Testament (recent editions)*

Aland, Kurt, Matthew Black, Bruce M. Metzger, and Allen Wikgren (eds.), *The Greek New Testament.* Stuttgart: United Bible Societies, 1966.

Nestle, Eberhard, *Novum Testamentum Graece,* 25th ed. by Erwin Nestle and Kurt Aland. Stuttgart: Württembergische Bibelanstalt, 1963.

Greek, Latin, English New Testament Students' Workbook (in addition to the Nestle Greek text this volume gives the Nestle Latin text together with the Confraternity of Christian Doctrine English translation of all the New Testament books — and a quarter of each page is left blank for the student to add notes and comment. Collegeville: Minnesota: The Liturgical Press).

C. *Grammars and Dictionaries*

Arndt-Gingrich, *A Greek-English Lexicon of the New Testament and Other Early Christian Literature.* Chicago: The University of Chicago Press.

Jay, Eric G., *New Testament Greek: An Introductory Grammar.* London: S. P. C. K., 1961.

Liddell, Henry George, and Robert Scott, *A Greek-English Lexicon.* New ed. (9th) by Henry Stuart Jones. Oxford: Clarendon Press, 1940. *Supplement,* ed. by E. A. Barber; Oxford: Clarendon Press, 1968.

Moulton, James Hope, W. F. Howard, and Nigel Turner Hitchin, *A Grammar of New Testament Greek.* 1: *Prolegomena* (3rd ed., 1957); 2: *Word Formation* (1960); 3: *Syntax, Sentence Building* 1963). Edinburgh: T. and T. Clark.

Moulton, William F., Alfred S. Geden, and Harold K. Moulton, *A Concordance to the Greek Testament, according to the Texts of Westcott and Hort, Tischendorf, and the English Revisers.* Edinburgh: T. and T. Clark, 1963.

D. *Synopses of the Gospels*

Aland, Kurt, *Synopsis of the Four Gospels: Greek-English Edition of the Synopsis Quattuor Evangeliorum.* Stuttgart: United Bible Societies, 1972.

Benoit, Pierre, and M.-E. Boismard. *Synopse des Quatre Evangiles.* Paris: Editions du Cerf, 1965.

E. *Some Commentaries on the Fourth Gospel*

Barrett, Charles Kingsley, *The Gospel according to St. John.* London: S. P. C. K., 1955.

Brown, Raymond E., *The Gospel according to John.* 2 vols.; Anchor Bible 29-30. Garden City, N.Y.: Doubleday, 1966-70.

Dodd, C. H., *The Interpretation of the Fourth Gospel.* Cambridge: Cambridge University Press, 1953.

Lagrange, Marie-Joseph, *Evangile selon S. Jean: Commentaire sur le texte grec.* Paris: Gabalda, 1936.

Schnackenburg, Rudolf, *The Gospel according to John.* 1, tr. from *Das Johannesevangelium* (Freiburg: Herder, 1965—). New York: Herder and Herder, 1968.

Malatesta, Edward, *St. John's Gospel 1920–1965: A Cumulative and Classified Bibliography of Books and Articles on the Fourth Gospel.* Rome: Pontifical Biblical Institute, 1967. Contains 3120 titles.

Introduction

Judeo-Christianity is the only "historical" religion in the sense that only in it did God reveal himself through events and especially through the "event which is Jesus Christ," an event that reached its climactic moment in the Resurrection.

God entered into human history by intervening in the life of Abraham and by calling Moses. He became fully present to us in Jesus Christ and is still constantly at work in history.

Christianity in its entirety is a "sacred history," that is, an historical process inspired by God: the advance of mankind through history to the parousia.

What a contrast with the religions of the East! For them, history is part of the realm of appearances and illusion from which man must extricate himself. Time and the world are only a mirage. The striving for mystical states is to liberate the soul from all that is contingent and allow it to achieve an identification with a universal soul and to lose itself in an undifferentiated absolute.

A basic question that we Christians must answer is: Is the alleged intervention of God in history something that really took place? In the attempt to answer the question, an indispensable first step is to ask and answer a basic question: Does the text of the New Testament have value as history?

The present essay will show that the fourth Gospel has an incomparable textual story and that the establishment of its text history provides us with highest assurance of its authenticity.

The original text, that is, the manuscript composed by the author of the fourth Gospel, is now lost and must in fact have disappeared quite early. That was the fate of all the writings of antiquity; with the exception of the Dead Sea scrolls we do not possess a single original manuscript from that period.

It is instructive to note that the oldest manuscripts of the great Greek tragedians, Aeschylus and Sophocles, date from the eleventh century, and the oldest manuscript of the Greek historian, Thucydides, from the tenth. Marcus Aurelius, who died in 180 A.D., was edited in 1559 on the basis of a manuscript that is now lost, and is represented today by a single manuscript from the fourteenth century. Of the Latin classical writers Virgil, who died in 19 B.C., has fared best; his works are preserved in a manuscript of the fourth or fifth century. (Editions of the classical writers will usually give this kind of information in their introductions.)

In the mid-nineteenth century, there was no talk yet of papyri. Moreover, the study of manuscripts had to be done where the manuscripts were kept, since photocopying had not yet become a business. In this area, as in so many others, historical research today has become, in comparison with past ages, an immensely easier matter; we can now study manuscripts and papyri from all over the world in microfilms that are sometimes clearer than the original document.

This availability enables us readily to follow the transmission of the biblical text stage by stage, as determined by the paleographers and papyrologists. We shall not, however, enter into the critical study of variant readings.

The Greek manuscripts of the New Testament that were known in 1958 numbered about 5000. Of these, 266 are written in majuscules or uncials; 2,754 are in minuscules; 1,838 are lectionaries containing passages from the Bible for use in the liturgy; 81 are papyri which for the most part contain only small fragments of the biblical text.

Chapter One

The Text of the Fourth Gospel from the Beginning of the Second Century to the Beginning of the Fourth

Papyrus, on which the Gospels were written, was not one of the nobler writing materials. In the various parts of the civilized east men in fact used many kinds of material for writing: stone, leaves, bark, wood, metals, linen, baked clay, and potsherds. But for the transmission of the Bible only three materials are really important: leather, papyrus, and parchment.

As for leather, we know that prepared skins had long been used as a writing material. In Egypt, some written documents dating back to the Fourth Dynasty (2000–1788 B.C.) have survived.

The lawbook called the Talmud was written on animal skins sewn together to form a roll. The rolls from the Dead Sea area were made of lamb skins or the skins of young goats. Copies of the Bible for reading in the synagogues normally were written on leather.

Papyrus was a much more commonly used material, derived from the papyrus plant of the Nile delta. The fibers of the stem of the plant were cut into narrow strips which were laid out in two layers crosswise to each other. The two layers were then tightly glued together in a press. The end-product was sheets of material that were fastened together to produce rolls of up to 35 feet in length.

Herodotus claims that any civilized people must use papyrus as the ordinary material for making books.

Against this background we can understand that when the Jews in Egypt during the third century B.C. commissioned a Greek translation of the Law and the prophets, they received a translation written on papyrus rolls. When the Gospels were written, between 65 and 100 A.D., papyrus was still the main material being used. It had many advantages, and the Greco-Roman world made use of it for a thousand years.

But, from our viewpoint, as we look back from a much later time, papyrus was not very durable; dampness destroyed it. Only in one country was the earth so dry that papyrus manuscripts had a chance of surviving. The country was Egypt.

The past hundred years have brought such papyri to light; previously it was believed that anything written on papyrus was gone forever. Ever since the last decades of the nineteenth century we have received a flood of light from the region of the Nile. The first really important discovery was made in 1877 when some natives of the Faiyum region sold a cache of papyri to Archduke Rainer of Austria; the papyri are now in the Vienna Library. Around this same time, Flinders Petrie, the English archeologist (1853–1942), found a lost play of Euripides in the paper used for wrapping mummies. E. Wallis Budge acquired Aristotle's treatise on the Athenian Constitution for the British Museum; Frederick Kenyon published it in 1891.

1. Biblical Papyri

The discoveries of the last fifty years have enabled us to add a new dimension to the transmission of the biblical text.

Philologists had previously supposed that the papyrus roll continued to be used until papyrus was replaced by leather. But we know now, as Professor Roberts of Oxford has shown in his study of the codex, that from the end of the first century Christian and pagan literature alike used a codex, not a roll. This means that the sheets of papyrus were folded in two, making four pages, and that quires or signatures of these were sewn together to form a book or codex.

The ancestor of the codex was the wooden or ivory tablet used for correspondence. The Romans soon shifted, however, to leather and then parchment. The links in the chain connecting the papyrus codex of Egypt with the parchment codex of Rome remain hypothetical.

Egypt was the granary for the Roman Empire (it was on a grain transport ship that St. Paul was shipwrecked near Malta), and Egyptian Christians maintained close connections with the Christians of Rome during the first century. It is not surprising then that we should find books of the New Testament in Egypt. In the mid-nineteenth century, however, the earliest text of the New Testament that we possessed was the Codex Vaticanus, a fine manuscript from the year 330. In the light of this fact, Baur's or Loisy's hypothesis that the fourth Gospel was composed no earlier than the mid-second century becomes more understandable. Even so, they too easily overlooked the fact that Paul's letters attest a highly developed body of doctrine only twenty years after the death of Jesus.

In 1920 the John Rylands Library at Manchester (plate 1) acquired some papyrus fragments from the Faiyum region of the Nile valley. Two Oxford scholars, Drs. Grenfell and Hunt, had begun publication of documents already in the Library's possession in 1913 and 1915. A third volume, the catalogue, was also to contain the fragments acquired in 1920.

In 1935, Professor Colin Henderson Roberts (born in 1909; fellow of St. John's College, Oxford; appointed professor of papyrology in 1937; fellow of the British Academy) published separately a small but priceless fragment of a papyrus codex. The fragment (plate 2) measures 8 cm by 6 cm and contains a text written in black ink on light colored papyrus. We hardly need say that present-day photography can bring out the blackness of the ink more sharply, while toning down the grayish-brown color of the papyrus as the naked eye sees it in the exposition case (plate 4).

The short text is part of a codex that included the fourth Gospel. It is the oldest known fragment of the New Testament and our earliest witness to the existence of the fourth Gospel. This claim is based solely on paleographical arguments, which are developed by Professor Roberts in his brochure on the fragment. It is interesting to note that the passage preserved contains Pilate's notorious question: "What is truth?"

We shall here simply refer to some dated papyri to which Papyrus 457 of Manchester shows striking resemblances; the reader may compare the reproductions. The first is a passage from the Iliad, which Wilhelm Schubart discusses in his book on the Greek papyri at Berlin. The fragment dates from the last decades of the first century; the passage is from Book 8, versus 436-447, while the verse at the bottom of the fragment is verse 434 (plate 6). The second text is Papyrus Egerton 2, which is conservatively dated as mid-second century.

In 1934 the British Museum acquired a parcel of Egyptian Christian papyri of unequal value; they were catalogued as "Egerton Papyri" after the name of the larger collection of which they are a part. The most notable of the papyri fragments is the one that interests us: Papyrus Egerton 2, which was edited with the rest of the parcel in 1935 in a book entitled *Fragments of an Unknown Gospel and Other Early Christian Papyri*.

The fragment consists of two leaves in fairly good condition and a damaged piece of a third. Plate 8 gives one side of one leaf. In translation it reads: "(Coming) to him, they tested him with questions, saying: 'Jesus, teacher, we know you come from God, for the things you do bear witness to it, far more than anything the prophets did. Tell us, therefore: May we render to kings what it is within their authority to ask? Shall we give it or not?' But Jesus, knowing their thoughts, was angry and said: 'Why do you pay me lip-service as "teacher" but not listen to what I say? Isaiah was right when he prophecied concerning you: "This people honors me with their lips, but their heart is far from me; their service is useless." ' " The text has parallels in Matthew 22:16-22; John 3:2; Matthew 15:7-8.

According to the editors, Bell and Skeat, who were curators of manuscripts in the British Museum, the papyri contained the text of an unknown, apocryphal gospel, or a "fifth gospel," as the newspaper accounts of the day put it. Even at that, the almost verbatim correspondence of the first half of the text to the Gospel of John and the less striking but nonetheless clear likeness of the second half to the Synoptics leaves many questions unanswered.

There can be no question here of a harmony of the four Gospels in the style of Tatian in his *Diatessaron*. What we have here, then, may well be a collection of extracts, a kind of anthology of episodes taken from the early oral tradition that anteceded the writing of our present Gospels, or from one of the collections to which Luke refers in his prologue. The paleographic evidence, according to Bell and Skeat, suggests a date of 150 at the latest for the papyrus.

Let us return to Professor Roberts. He confirms his own paleographical analysis with the help of two papyri that can be dated rather accurately. These help situate Manchester Papyrus 457 quite precisely.

The first is a lament written, under the emperor Trajan (98–117), in a firm but not especially beautiful hand; the formation of the letters is comparable to that found in Manchester Papyrus 457 (plate 10). The second is a piece of writing from Hadrian's official chancery (plate 12); W. Schubart dates this as 135 A.D.; again, the formation of the letters resembles that of Manchester Papyrus 457.

We may end these comparisons which help date the Manchester papyrus by setting it alongside Manchester Papyrus 544, a fragment of the Iliad, Book 24, lines 169-176. This latter contains 35 letters distributed over eight lines (plate 12). Let the reader examine the transcription of the 35 letters and the complete text of these verses of the Iliad. These 35 letters can be assigned without any hesitation to the beginning of the second century.

2. PAPYRUS BODMER II

A sensational discovery in the area of biblical papyri was published in 1956, with a supplement following in 1962. It was the Papyrus Bodmer II.

The Martin Bodmer library is a treasure house of ancient literature. Victor Martin, of the University of Geneva, and J. W. B. Barns, professor of papyrology at Oxford, in 1962 published a complete reproduction of a papyrus of the fourth Gospel which dates from not later than 200. From a specimen page (plate 16) we can see how the first fourteen chapters have been preserved in a continuous text; the reconstruction of chapter 18, verses 37-40 (plate 18), which corresponds to Manchester

Papyrus 457, gives an idea of the value of the fragments left of the last six chapters.

Papyrus Bodmer II is a codex, that is, a book formed from sets of leaves that were folded in half and placed one inside the other. This manner of using papyrus goes back to the first century, as Professor Roberts' study proves.

By the end of the third century the handiness and durability of the codex had assured its use, in preference to the roll, for every kind of writing. The Christian communities played an important part in establishing this preference because they adopted the codex for copies of the Gospels. The oldest fragment of a Gospel that we have is from a codex: Manchester Papyrus 456. The Chester Beatty papyri from the third century are likewise in codex form.

Papyrus had been used for such collections of writings ever since writing had been practiced in Egypt. In the west, parchment, though more expensive, was readily available; but in Egypt papyrus predominated. (In the light of the discoveries made in our century, there is no basis for pairing papyrus with roll and parchment with codex.)

Papyrus Bodmer II contains a substantial, and exceptionally well preserved, portion of a codex of 108 consecutive pages, measuring 16.2 cm by 14.2 cm, almost square in shape, easy to handle and easy to carry. Papyrus 457 of Manchester was part of a codex that probably contained 130 pages.

Professor Martin has made a detailed analysis of the handwriting. It is highly stylized and merits the description "literary." The so-called biblical uncial hand of the Codex Sinaiticus (clearly discernible in the photographic enlargement, plate 28) is simply a variation on the hand in Papyrus Bodmer II; the variation is due in part to the fact that the Sinaiticus is written on parchment, which offers a better surface for the pen. The writing in Manchester Papyrus 457 and in Papyrus Egerton 2 is essentially the same.

Professor Martin, who has submitted his papyrus to scrutiny by other experts, attributes this copy of the Gospel of John to the year 200; this makes it more than a century older than Vaticanus and Sinaiticus. It contains hardly any punctuation. The interested reader can follow Professor Martin in his detailed study of the paleographic evidence.

3. Papyrus 75

In 1961 another sensation shook the world of papyrology: the Bodmer Library published Bodmer XIV and XV, which was given the number 75 in the series of biblical papyri. Here we have a goodly part of the Gospel of Luke and the first thirteen chapters of John.

This papyrus is as old as — perhaps even older than — Bodmer II. The hand is a neat vertical uncial that evidently belongs to the imperial period and can be dated between 175 and 225.

The edition by Miss Bongard has thirty pages describing the characteristics of the manuscript. One page is reproduced in Plate 20; it is a page from a codex that, when intact, must have contained 144 pages (36 sheets folded in half).

Study of the available papyri shows that at the time when they were written there was no complete and fixed method of subdivision. Moreover, the three papyri, while having the same geographical origin and being written in the same period, do not show a uniform text; it follows that there was no single authoritative recension of the Gospels in Egypt. We must bear in mind that Christians in the Mediterranean world copied the Gospels with great frequency; we must therefore expect to find the text more fluid than would be the case with the great works of literature.

4. THE CHESTER BEATTY COLLECTION

In the London *Times* of November 19, 1931, Sir Frederic George Kenyon, former Director of the British Museum, announced the discovery of a very important batch of Greek biblical papyri. In 1933 he began publication of the series. Mr. A. Chester Beatty, an American collector, had bought the papyri in 1930 from Egyptian sellers whose identity is unknown, and handed them over for study to three specialists in papyrology: Kenyon and Bell, along with Ibscher of Berlin.

The batch contained over 200 papyrus leaves, the debris of about a dozen ancient manuscripts. Some time later, Mr. Beatty acquired 46 more leaves from the same source.

In 1932–33 the University of Michigan acquired about 30 leaves which belonged with the batch Mr. Beatty had bought. Two of them, parts of a manuscript containing the Gospels and the Acts of the Apostles, became part of the Chester Beatty collection; the rest, which contained a good part of the Letters of St. Paul, were edited in 1935 by H. A. Sanders, a member of the University.

Finally, the National Library at Vienna had acquired some fragments of Matthew that belonged to the same original set. They were edited by H. Gerstinger in 1933. Thus, probably for commercial reasons, the earlier owner of these papyri had divided them up among several buyers. The whole collection, however, though now divided among various owners, is known as the Chester Beatty Papyri.

The manuscripts come from Egypt, from the area west of the Nile, in Upper Egypt, where great numbers of papyri have been found, especially at Madinet and El Faiyum and at the ancient Oxyrhynchus (modern El Bahnasa). The original source cannot be pinpointed more closely.

More important than the geographical origin is the contents of these manuscripts. They contain: (1) the Gospels and Acts: 30 leaves out of the 110 the manuscript would normally have had; (2) Letters of St. Paul: 86

leaves of the approximately one hundred that would have been required for the whole Pauline corpus; (3) Apocalypse: 10 leaves; (4) Old Testament: more than 150 leaves.

With the help of the transcription (plate 25) examine the example given of these papyri (plate 24). Basing their judgment on the writing, the material, and comparisons with dated manuscripts, paleographers agree in regarding the papyri as written between 200 and 250.

Let us pause here before moving on to the next and very important category of manuscripts: the uncials.

Quite divergent dates have been suggested for the composition of the Fourth Gospel: Bruno Bauer, around 160–170; Ernest Renan, between 110 and 115; Alfred Loisy, between 100 and 125; Adolf von Harnack, about 80–110. The discovery of the papyri provides an extraordinary external confirmation of the position von Harnack had reached through internal criticism.

The Egerton Papyrus shows that a text of the Fourth Gospel resembling the one we now have had reached Egypt before 150. It would, however, take a certain amount of time for a writing composed at Ephesus to reach Upper Egypt, and we are forced to assign the composition of the Fourth Gospel, in its present form, to around 100, that is, to around the traditional date. Rylands Papyrus 457 dates from the very generation during which the Fourth Gospel was redacted, and proves beyond doubt that this Gospel existed and was in circulation in the first half of the second century.

The very fact that so old a fragment was found in a relatively remote part of Upper Egypt (at Oxyrhynchus) cuts the ground out from under those scholars who would assign the Gospel a rather late origin. And there are other points that deserve emphasis. For example, the Rylands and Egerton Papyri are fragments of codexes, not of rolls. In addition, the Egerton Papyrus supposes that the writer had before him both the Synoptic Gospels and the Fourth Gospel.

Although the papyri discovered in the twentieth century do not modify our knowledge of the Gospel text, they are nonetheless very important on several counts. The sheer quantity of documents discovered is already noteworthy — almost 300 biblical papyri pages in the Chester Beatty collection alone — but the most important aspect of the discoveries is the early date of the papyri. The oldest text of the Gospels that we now have belongs to the first half of the second century, thus bringing us 200 years closer than heretofore to apostolic times and leaving us within about thirty years from the time of their composition. Furthermore, the papyri have deepened our confidence in our present text of the Gospels, for we now find that the text has been transmitted in its integrity since the beginning of the second century. There are variants, of course, but they do not change the content of the texts.

For many years, the date of the Fourth Gospel was hotly debated by historians and exegetes; now, the traditional date of 95, which Harnack defended, has been confirmed by philological facts.

Bibliography on the Papyri

I. *General Bibliography*
Bataille, André, "Papyrologie," in Charles M. D. Samarin (ed.), *L'histoire et ses méthodes.* Paris: Gallimard, 1961. Pp. 498-527.
———, *Les Papyrus.* Paris: Presses Universitaires de France, 1955.
———, *Pour une terminologie en paléographie grecque.* Paris: Klincksieck, 1954.
Botte, Bernard, "Papyrus bibliques," *Dictionnaire de la Bible: Supplément* 6 (Paris: Letouzey et Ané, 1960) 1109-1120.
David, Martin, and Bernard Abraham Van Groningen, *Papyrological Primer.* 4th ed. Leiden: Brill, 1965.
Hombert, Marcel, "Chronique d'Egypte: L'état des études de papyrologie au lendemain de la guerre," *Revue des études grecques*, 1947–48.
Kenyon, Frederic George, *The Paleography of Greek Papyri.* Oxford: Clarendon Press, 1899.
———, and H. I. Bell, *Catalogue of the Greek Papyri in the British Museum.* 6 vols. London, 1911.
Leclercq, Henri, "Papyrus," *Dictionnaire d'archéologie chrétienne et de liturgie* 13 (Paris: Letouzey et Ané, 1937) 1370-1520.
Liddell, Henry George, and Robert Scott, *A Greek-English Lexicon.* New (9th) ed. by Henry Stuart Jones. Oxford: Clarendon Press, 1940. Pp. xliii-xlv: list of publications on the papyri.
Page, D. L., *Select Papyri.* 3 vols. London: Heineman, 1942-50.
Papyri Selectae, compiled and edited by E. Boswinkel, P. J. Sijpedteijn, P. W. Pestman, and P. L. Bat. Leiden: Brill, 1965.
Peremans, Willy, and Jozef Vergote, *Papyrologisch Handboek.* Louvain: 1942.
Preisendanz, Karl, *Papyrusfunde und Papyrusforschung.* Leipzig: Hiersemann, 1946.
Roberts, Colin Henderson, *Greek Literary Hands. (350 B.C.–400 A.D.).* Oxford Paleographical Handbook. Oxford: Clarendon Press, 1956.
Schubart, Wilhelm, *Einführung in die Papyruskunde.* 3rd ed. Leipzig: Teubner, 1927.
Turner, Gardner Eric, *Greek Papyri: An Introduction.* Oxford: Clarendon Press, 1968.
A. Aland, Kurt, *Kurzgefasste Liste der griechischen Handschriften des Neuen Testamentes.* Berlin: De Gruyter, 1963. Pp. 29-33 contain a list of the papyri which have passages of the New Testament. The dates have been established by Herbert Hunger (Vienna), Karl Preisendanz (Heidelberg), Colin Henderson Roberts (Oxford), Wilhelm Schubart (Halle), and Theodore Cussy Skeat (London). These paleographers base their judgment on the whole of the corpus of New Testament Greek papyri. Cf. Kurt Aland, "Neue Neutestamentliche Papyri II," *New Testament Studies* 9 (1962–63) 303-16.
B. Mayser, Edwin, *Grammatik der griechischen Papyri aus der Ptolemäerzeit*, I/1: *Laut- und Wortlehre* (new ed., 1923); I/2: *Flexionslehre* (2nd ed., 1938); I/3: *Stammbildung* (1935); II/1: *Satzlehre* (1926); II/2: *Satzlehre* (1934); II/3 *Satzlehre* (1934). Leipzig: Teubner. The basic aid for understanding the texts.
II. *Special Bibliography*
A. Papyrus 457 of Manchester
Catalogue of the Greek Papyri in the John Rylands Library. 1: *Literary Texts (nos. 1–61)*, ed. by Arthur S. Hunt (1911); 2: *Documents of the Ptolemaic and Roman Periods (nos. 62-456)*, ed. by J. M. Johnson, Victor Martin, and Arthur S. Hunt (1915); 3: *Theological and Literary Texts* (nos. 457-551), ed. by Colin Henderson Roberts (1938); 4: *Documents of the Ptolemaic, Roman, and Byzantine Periods (nos. 552-717)*, ed. by Colin Henderson Roberts and E. G. Turner (1952). Manchester: Manchester University Press.
Roberts, Colin Henderson, *An Unpublished Fragment of the Fourth Gospel in the John Rylands Library: Chapter XVIII, verses 31-34, 37-38.* Manchester: Manchester University Press, 1935. *Reviews:* H. I. Bell, *Journal of Egyptian Archaeology* 21 (1935)

266-67; P. Benoit, *Revue biblique* 45 (1936) 269-72; G. Ghedini, *Aegyptus* 15 (1935) 425-26; J. Jeremias, *Theologische Blätter* 15 (1936) 97-100; H. Lietzmann, *Zeitschrift für die neutestamentliche Wissenschaft* 34 (1935) 285; A. Merk, *Biblica* 17 (1936) 99-101.

B. Egerton 2

Bell, H. I., and T. C. Skeat, *Fragments of an Unknown Gospel and Other Early Christian Papyri*. London: British Museum, 1935.

    Reviews and Studies: L. Cerfaux, "L'evangile inconnu," in his *Etudes d' exégèse et d'histoire religieuse* (3 vols. Gembloux: Duculot, 1954-62), 1:279-99; M. Goguel, "Les fragments nouvellement découverts d'un évangile du deuxième siècle," *Revue d'histoire et de littérature religieuse* 15 (1935) 465; J. Huby, "Une importante découverte papyrologique," *Etudes* 224 (1935) 763-75; G. Mayeda, *Das Leben Jesu: Fragment Papyrus Egerton 2 und seine Stellung in der urchristlichen Literaturegeschichte* (Bern: P. Haupt, 1946); E. R. Smothers, "Un nouvelle évangile du deuxième siècle," *Recherches de science religieuse* 25 (1935) 358-62; H. Vogel, *Theologische Rundschau* 34 (1935) 315.

C. Papyrus Bodmer II

Martin, Victor, and J. W. B. Barns, *Evangile de Jean (I-XIV): Papyrus Bodmer II*. Geneva: Bibliotheca Bodmeriana, 1956.

————, *Evangile de Jean (XVI-XII): Papyrus Bodmer II*. Geneva: Bibliotheca Bodmeriana, 1958.

——, *Evangile de Jean (I-XXI): Papyrus Bodmer II*. New enlarged and revised ed. Geneva: Bibliotheca Bodmeriana, 1962.

    Reviews and Studies: K. Aland, "Papyrus Bodmer II: Ein erster Bericht," *Theologische Literaturzeitung* 82 (1957) 161-84; J. B. Bauer, "Zur Datierung des Papyrus Bodmer II," *Biblische Zeitschrift* 12 (1968) 121-22 ("mid-second century"); M..-E. Boismard, "Le papyrus Bodmer II," *Review biblique* 64 (1957) 363-97; M.-E. Boismard and G. Roux, "Papyrus Bodmer II," *Revue biblique* 70 (1963) 120-33; F.-M. Braun, "Un nouveau papyrus johannique: Le papyrus Bodmer II," *Revue Thomiste* 57 (1957) 79-86; B. Brinkmann, "Eine Papyrus-Handschrift des Johannesevangeliums aus dem 2. Jahrhundert," *Scholastik* 32 (1957) 399-410.

D. Papyrus Bodmer XV

Martin, Victor, and Rodolphe Kasser, *Papyrus Bodmer XV: Evangile de Jean, C. 1–15*. Geneva: Bibliotheca Bodmeriana, 1961.

    Reviews and Studies: Ph.-H. Menoud, "Papyrus Bodmer XV," *Revue de théologie et de philosophie* 12 (1962) 107-16; C. L. Porter, "Papyrus Bodmer XV and the Text of Codex Vaticanus," *Journal of Biblical Literature* 81 (1962) 363-76.

E. The Chester Beatty Papyri

Kenyon, Frederic George, *The Chester Beatty Biblical Papyri: Descriptions and Texts of Twelve Manuscripts on Papyrus of the Greek Bible*. Fasc. II: *The Gospels and Acts*. London: Emery Walker, 1933. From 1933 to 1941 15 fascicles were published.

Beatty, Afred Chester, *The Chester Beatty Library*, Dublin: Emery Walker, 1958.

    Reviews and Studies: M. Fischen, *Studien zu den Evangelien der Chester Beatty Papyri* (University of Breslau Dissertations, no. 120; presented May 10, 1937); H. W. Huston, *Journal of Biblical Literature* 74 (1955) 262-71; W. G. Kümmel, *Theologische Rundschau* 10 (1938) 292-98 (excellent survey of studies published 1933-38 on the Chester Beatty Papyri); M. J. Lagrange, "Les papyrus Chester Beatty pour les Evangiles," *Revue biblique* 43 (1934) 5-41; C. C. Tarelli, *Journal of Theological Studies* 40 (1939) 46; and 41 (1940) 253-60.

F. The Nomina Sacra: The sacred names are contracted in the biblical papyri and other manuscripts, especially from the third century on. *Kurios* = KC, *Jesus* = IC, *Huios* = YC, each abbreviation having a bar across the top of the letters.

Boll, Franz, "Einleitung" to Ludwig Traube's *Vorlesungen und Abhandlungen*. 3 vols. Munich: Beck, 1909–20.

Paap, A. H. R. E., *Nomina Sacra in the Greek Papyri of the First Five Centuries A.D.: The Sources and Some Deductions* (Papyrologica Lugduno-Batava 8). Leiden: Brill, 1959.

Nachmanson, E. "Contraction of the Nomina Sacra (Greek Inscriptions)," *Eranos* 10 (1910) 101-44.

Chapter Two

Fourth Gospel Manuscripts
from the Fourth
to the Ninth Centuries

1. The Uncial Manuscripts

After the beginning of the fourth century the Bible was copied on parchment or animal skins (sheep, lamb, calf) prepared according to a method invented at Pergamum in the second century B.C. Pliny the Elder tells the story in his *Natural History* (XIII, 21). According to legend, Eumenes of Pergamum invented parchment when the Ptolemies, jealous of book collectors, put an embargo on the export of papyrus.

This very strong material had earlier been quite costly but in the fourth century it became so cheap that it everywhere replaced the much more delicate papyrus. The sheets were folded to form codexes or books, and sewn together by way of binding.

Capital letters were used in writing on parchment; initially they were square in shape, like the letters used in epigraphs, but later on they became rounded or uncial.

The most recent list of biblical uncial manuscripts published by Kurt Aland contains 266 entries. The following will be discussed here (the plates contain a sample, with transcription, of each): Codex Vaticanus, Codex Sinaiticus, Codex Ephraemi Rescriptus; Codex Alexandrinus, Codex Bezae, Codex Freer (Washington), Codex Koridethi, the Caesarea Codex, and Codex WN of Vienna.

2. Codex Vaticanus

The uncial writing of the fourth century, quite familiar to scholars today, is especially elegant in Vaticanus as the reproduction clearly shows (plate 24). Column 2 has been transcribed (plate 25) in capital letters to facilitate the reading of verses 28-36, while column 3 is presented in the usual Greek type.

Each page of the Codex has three columns of text, and each column has forty-two lines. The parchment is of very good quality. Initial letters are not larger than the other characters, but the first letter of a chapter either protrudes into the margin a bit or is preceded by a space, as in the twenty-ninth line of column 3 (plate 24) where there is a space before the letter T in the first word of chapter 19 (the figure in the right-hand margin of the column is a later addition).

The first copyist used no accents or breathing marks; punctuation is rare and is usually replaced by a slight space between words.

The actual size of the square pages is 27 to 28 cm on a side. The manuscript contains 759 leaves, 617 for the Old Testament and 142 for the New. Two correctors must have worked on the original copy, the first probably a contemporary of the copyist, the second probably belonging to the eleventh or twelfth century. Tischendorf was of the opinion that the manuscript was copied in the same scriptorium as Codex Sinaiticus; this is a possibility, but no more than a possibility.

The Codex was given its present serial number (Vatican Greek 1209) only in the time of Paul V (1605–21). A photographic reproduction was made at Milan from 1902 to 1906. A quite recent edition of remarkable clarity enables us to study the text at every point with great ease.

The manuscript is of prime importance in establishing the Greek text of the Bible.

3. CODEX SINAITICUS

Sinai and Horeb are the two names the Israelites gave to the mountain on which Yahweh made his presence known to Moses and concluded his covenant with Israel. Mt. Sinai is not an isolated mountain but rather a mountain mass from which emerge peaks of from 2000 to 2600 meters in height.

It is a jumble of rocks, with jagged ridges and bizarre looking peaks, furrowed in every direction by twisting valleys and long narrow strips of flat open country, and riven by rough gorges and precipitous ravines.

At the foot of Gebel Musa (2244 m) nestles the monastery of St. Catherine. From the fourth century on, early Christian hermits lived in great numbers in the caves of the area. Their place of gathering at that time was a little church consecrated to the Virgin. Time and again in the course of the fourth and fifth centuries desert brigands killed the solitary monks, until finally Emperor Justinian had a church built with a fortified enclosure around it. Within this enclosure the wretched buildings of the community — cells and outbuildings — were erected at random. Like monasteries generally, this one had a library with an adjoining scriptorium where monks copied manuscripts.

The library at Mt. Sinai today contains 3300 manuscripts — Greek Syriac, Arabic, Slavonic — that are extremely important for our knowledge of the Bible. The Greek manuscripts are in the majority, numbering over 1500; Victor Gardthausen published a catalogue of them at Oxford in 1866.

For centuries all these philological treasures gathered dust there, unknown to the world of scholarship and unused by the monks who were ignorant of their value. Then, in 1958, a scientific expedition, sponsored by the University of Michigan and Princeton University, came to photograph the mosaics, frescoes, icons, and illuminated manuscripts. It was following directly upon an expedition of 1950, sponsored by the Library of Congress, which had microfilmed a great number of manuscripts and thus made them accessible to the scholars of the world.

We, however, are interested in the events of a much earlier time: the spring of 1844. In that year, Lobegott Friedrich Konstantin von Tischendorf, a great German scholar in the field of biblical criticism, visited the monastery of St. Catherine and while there discovered forty-three detached pages being used as waste paper to light a stove in his room. He took them with him back to Leipzig, where they now belong to the University Library, and edited them in a book entitled *Codex Frederico-Augustanus* (Leipzig, 1846), in honor of Frederick Augustus, king of Saxony, who had financed his mission to Sinai.

Tischendorf returned to Mt. Sinai in 1853, but it was only in 1859 that there fell into his hands 199 pages of the Old Testament and the complete New Testament. He and some university students began to transcribe the texts; then, in September, 1859, the monks gave him permission to take the precious manuscript to Europe for editing (cf. plates 27 and 31). This was done in 1862, but Tischendorf gave the manuscript to Tsar Alexander II of Russia. In 1869 the manuscript passed from the archives of the minister of foreign affairs to the Library of St. Petersburg. Did the monks in their naivete simply relinquish their treasure? The Russians, at least, claimed that the monks had given it to the Tsar, and that in return the Tsar made an offering of 7000 rubles.

The definitive publication of the codex had to wait until the twentieth century when the Oxford University Press issued a facsimile of photographs taken by Kirsopp Lake (New Testament, 1911; Old Testament, 1922).

In 1933, after the Russian Revolution, the U.S.S.R., which had no interest in the Bible and needed money, negotiated the sale of the Codex to the British Museum for 100,000 pounds sterling. The British government advanced half of the money, and the rest was raised by a nation-wide appeal. Before Christmas, 1933, the manuscript was brought to London under heavy guard.

The romantic story of Codex Sinaiticus eventually caused Tischendorf some painful moments. From 1856 on, a clever Greek Constantine Simonides, was stirring up the waters by forging manuscripts of supposedly fabulous antiquity: a Homer written in a prehistoric hand, a copy of the Gospel of Matthew on papyrus that was written fifteen years after the Ascension, and so forth.

The swindler had his moment of glory, for among the scholars dealing with Simonides was Tischendorf. Simonides had a delightful plan for gaining revenge: he proudly admitted his authorship of the forgeries but then asserted that one of his forgeries had actually been accepted by all as an ancient document: the Codex Sinaiticus whose discovery Tischendorf had so triumphantly proclaimed!

In any event Tischendorf had not been quite straightforward. In 1964, Igor Sevcenko, of Columbia University, published in *Scriptorium* some new documents on Tischendorf and the Sinaiticus that demythologize the melodramatic story of Tischendorf's discovery of the famous manuscript. Tischendorf already knew the origin of the first 43 pages that he published at Leipzig, but kept the secret until he was able to bring the other 346 pages back to Europe. Porfirij Uspenskij, a Russian scholar, had already seen, in 1845, a copy of the Septuagint in the monastery of St. Catherine; several letters attest this, and it happened before Tischendorf's visit. Tischendorf emerges as a boastful, excitable, and occasionally dishonest fellow; he lessens the honor of German philology, and the Russian scholar gains by it. As a result, the legend is tarnished, but the manuscript remains no less unique.

Back to Simonides' claim. Internal evidence alone would be enough to refute it. In addition, he could not have produced the 346 pages of the Sinaiticus in the time he says it took him; furthermore, he would have had to have a rather remarkable copy in front of him to serve as a model.

When the Codex reached England in 1933, H. J. M. Milne and T. C. Skeat began a complete paleographical study. The results were published in 1938, in a volume called *Scribes and Correctors of the Codex Sinaiticus*. Milne and Skeat applied a new technique for the reading of ancient manuscripts: the use of ultraviolet lamps, and discovered the decorative lines at the end of each section and especially at the end of the Fourth Gospel. They also discovered the various correctors, the signs used for abbreviations, and the colophons or notations of the scribes at the end of books.

The dimensions of the manuscript pages are notable: approximately 38.5 by 34.5 cm. There are four columns to a page, and the square letters are from 4 to 5 mm in size.

In Plate 28, a passage containing some of the verses also found in Manchester Papyrus 457 is shown in twice its real size. Each reader, with the help of the transcription, will be able to see for himself what an aid photography is to the philologist who wishes to study the additions to the text.

Here, then, we have a complete Greek text of the Bible that was unknown to philologists only a century ago!

4. CODEX EPHRAEMI RESCRIPTUS

The manuscript of this name is number 9 in the Greek collection at the National Library in Paris; it was no. 1905 in the Bibliothèque du Roi and no. 3769 in the Bibliothèque de Colbert.

It is a palimpsest, that is, a manuscript from which the original writing was scraped away so that a new text might be written. In the Middle Ages the scarcity of parchment made palimpsests common.

The original writing was in a fifth-century uncial hand, and the text consisted of Job, Proverbs, Qoheleth, the Song of Songs, Wisdom, Sirach, the four Gospels, the Acts of the Apostles, the Letters of Paul, the Catholic Letters, and the Apocalypse.

The later writing is in a thirteenth-century cursive hand, and the text is the twenty-three discourses or treatises of St. Ephraem the Syrian, in a Greek translation.

In all there are 209 palimpsest pages, with a single column of biblical text to a page. The pages average 41 lines to the column; some have 40 or 42, 4 have 46. The specimen in Plate 32 has 41.

The characters are larger and more carefully made than in Vaticanus and Sinaiticus. The uncial is almost as tall as the nail on a man's little finger. In form, being bound into a fixed book, the codex resembles the Codes Alexandrinus.

The manuscript was probably written before the middle of the fifth century, certainly in Egypt, perhaps at Alexandria. It contains corrections from the sixth and ninth centuries. The age has been established from the shape of the letters, the indications given for chapters and section, the sequence of the Pauline Letters, the signatures, and the methods of the two correctors.

In the sixteenth century the manuscript belonged to Cardinal Ridolfi at Florence; on his death it was bought by the Strozzi (Florence), and later came into the hands of Queen Catherine de Medicis, finally coming to rest in Paris.

Montfaucon studied it and published a facsimile of it in his *Palaeographia Graeca* (1708). It was partially collated by Jean Boivin, X. Wetstein, Griesbach, Scholz, and Fleck, and completely collated by Tischendorf who edited it at Leipzig, 1843–45. His edition, however, is clear evidence of how difficult it is to decipher the writing. A serious revision would result if our modern photographic techniques (ultraviolet or infrared light) were applied.

Plates 32 and 33 show chapter 18 of the Fourth Gospel and a transcription.

5. CODEX ALEXANDRINUS

This manuscript, one of the most famous of the Greek Bible, belongs to the British Museum in London. As in the other manuscripts we have been discussing, the writing is uncial, and paleographers assign it to the fifth century. The whole is divided into gatherings of eight pages each, each page having two columns of text, and each column 49 to 51 lines. Plate 34 reproduces the page containing John 18:25–19:10; here each column has fifty-one lines.

Large initial letters, set in the margin, indicate the beginnings of paragraphs or sections. There are no accents and no breathing marks; all punctuation is indicated by a simple dot.

Each page is 32 cm in height, 26.3 in width. The whole manuscript, which is divided into four volumes, contains 773 pages: 630 for the Old Testament, 143 for the New. Some fragments are missing, especially in the Gospel of John, but all lacunae seem to be accidental.

The New Testament contains, in addition to the canonical text, the two Letters of St. Clement. The Old Testament used to have with it the apocryphal Psalms of Solomon; they are missing now but are indicated in the table of contents.

The manuscript is assigned to the fifth century, and there are good reasons for thinking that it was copied in Egypt. From the end of the eleventh century (1098) it belonged to the treasury of the Patriarch of Alexandria, as we are informed by a notation in Arabic at the bottom of the first page of Genesis. It came into the hands of Cyril Lucar (died 1638), Patriarch of Constantinople (1620ff.), while he was Patriarch of Alexandria (1602–20). He in turn made a present of it, in 1628, to Charles I, king of England, through the king's ambassador in Constantinople, Sir Thomas Roe.

The British Museum successfully undertook a photographic reproduction of the entire manuscript; generally speaking, it is this facsimile that scholars must consult.

6. Codex Bezae

This magnificent bilingual (Greek and Latin) manuscript of the Gospels and the Acts of the Apostles belongs to the Cambridge University Library. The writing extends across the page (rather than being in columns), with Greek and Latin texts on facing pages (Greek on the left, Latin on the right).

The parchment, which is of average quality, is divided into gatherings of eight pages. The manuscript originally had 534 pages, but now has only 406. Each page has thirty-three lines and measures 26 cm by 21.5 cm. (Note that the page has been reduced in size in Plate 36.)

The text, both Greek and Latin, is divided into paragraphs, and is the oldest manuscript of the New Testament to show this "stichometric" division. The manuscript was written in the sixth century in an uncial hand, without separation of words (except in titles) and without any punctuation except for a period at the end of each paragraph. The initial letter of each paragraph projects into the margin but is not decorate nor greatly enlarged. The first three lines of each book are written in red ink, as are the final signatures.

Indication of sections has been added by a second hand during the ninth century; a more recent hand has made marginal notations for the beginnings and endings of the liturgical pericopes.

The handwriting in both Greek and Latin is sufficiently alike that it could be the work of a single scribe. The text has undergone numerous corrections; scholars see as many as eight different hands from various periods changing the original text to the point of making it illegible in places. The oldest of these hands is that of the copyist himself.

Plate 36 reproduces a photograph from Cambridge and is exceptionally clear.

We must bear in mind that the Codex Bezae is a bilingual manuscript and that, like other bilingual uncial manuscripts, it provides a somewhat artificial text. This is because the copyist has been careful to make the Greek conform as closely as possible to the Latin, instead of, if anything, adapting the Latin to the Greek. This general observation does not, however, apply equally to all the variants in the manuscript. Westcott and Hort judged that the Codex Bezae gives us an unadulterated text of the "western" family; it is a late text, since it belongs paleographically to the sixth century, but an uncorrupt text, and one that is substantially a western text of the second century with a few accidental readings, probably of the fourth century.

Westcott and Hort add that despite a very large number of errors the manuscript is invaluable for the reconstruction of the authentic text and that, more than any other extant Greek manuscript, it gives a faithful image of the Gospels and Acts as generlly read in the third century and perhaps even in the second.

Codex Bezae must have been written in the west, but there is no description of it until the Renaissance. Theodore Beza, a French Calvinist (born at Vézelay, June 24, 1519; died at Geneva, October 13, 1615), used this manuscript in the second edition of his Greek New Testament (1582), calling it "my oldest copy." A year earlier, he had given it to Cambridge University, where it still bears his name: Codex Bezae.

7. Codex Freer of Washington, D. C.

This is the most important uncial manuscript to be discovered in the twentieth century. It contains the Gospels. Charles L. Freer, of Detroit, bought it in Egypt in 1906, and it is now in the Freer Museum of the Smithsonian Institute at Washington. The four Gospels are copied in the order that was customary in the west (see Codex Bezae): Matthew, John, Luke, Mark.

The manuscript seems to date from the end of the fourth century or the beginning of the fifth (cf. plate 28). The text is quite varied since it derives from copies of various manuscripts; it contains numerous iota-cisms.

After Mark 16:14, there is a remarkable insertion, part of which was also quoted by St. Jerome. The passage is as follows: "And they [the Twelve] said in their own defense: 'This wicked and unbelieving age is under the domination of Satan, and he does not allow anything under the yoke of the unclean spirits to grasp the truth and power of God. Therefore, show us your justice!' They spoke thus to Christ, and Christ answered them: 'The limit of the years of Satan's power has been fulfilled, but other fearful things are at hand. And I have been handed over to death for the sake of those who have sinned, so that they might be converted to the truth and sin no more but rather inherit the spiritual and incorruptible glory of heavenly righteousness.' "

According to Henry A. Sanders, in his edition of the text, the presence of different types of text is to be explained by the assumption that the codex derives from an earlier text that was itself made up of fragments from various manuscripts of the Gospels that were put together after Emperor Diocletian had tried to crush Christianity by destroying its sacred books. We may accept the hypothesis for what it is worth.

The manuscript contains 187 parchment pages, the dimensions of which are approximately 21 cm by 15 cm.

8. CODEX KORIDETHI

This codex was discovered in 1906 by Hermann von Soden in the church of Sts. Kerykos and Julitta at Koridethi. It is a manuscript of the Gospels but is odd in appearance, being written in late, rough uncials by a scribe who knew little Greek. It belonged to the monastery of Koridethi near the Caspian Sea, and is now in the State Museum at Tiflis. It can only be assigned a rather vague date, somewhere from the seventh to the ninth centuries inclusive. No other specimen of the same writing has ever been found.

The story of the discovery reminds us a bit of Tischendorf and Sinaiticus. As early as 1853 a Colonel Bartholomew had seen the manuscript at Swanetia, a mountainous area on the southern slope of the Caucasus. In 1869 the military governor of Kutaisi had temporary possession of it, it was then taken to St. Petersburg, but later returned to the Caucasus; it then disappeared for about thirty years, until it was rediscovered by Bishop Kirion and located for good at Tiflis.

Textual critics have assigned it the name Theta (eighth letter of the Greek alphabet). It has two columns to the page, and measures 28 cm high by 23 cm wide. The words are run together; there are accents, but few breathing marks.

P. Blake photographed the whole manuscript and gave the photographs to the Pierpont Morgan Collection of the Harvard College Library (see plate 42).

9. THE CAESAREA CODEX

The portion discovered at Caesarea in Cappadocia in 1896 is in the Leningrad Library. This sixth-century manuscript measures 32 cm by 26.5 cm, and has two columns of sixteen lines on each page. The parchment is tinted purple, and the sacred names are written in silver or gold. Other pages of the same manuscript are to be found in the monastery of St. John on Patmos, in the Vatican Library, the British Museum, and the National Library in Vienna (see plate 40).

10. CODEX WN OF THE NATIONAL LIBRARY IN VIENNA

This codex, belonging to the seventh century, contains only four leaves, each with two columns of twenty-four lines, and measuring 32.5 cm by 24.5 cm. It is written in brown ink (see plate 44).

The words are not separated; the use of accents and breathing marks follows no evident pattern, and the punctuation is special. Crosses are used to separate phrases, and there are notations for reading and singing.

Bibliography on the Uncial Manuscripts

I. *General Bibliography*
  A. Manuscripts in general
      Botte, Bernard, "Manuscrits grecs bibliques," *Dictionnaire de la Bible: Supplément* 5 (1957) 819-35.
      Dain, Alphonse, *Les manuscrits* (Paris: Les Belles Lettres, 1964). Excellent introduction to whole study of manuscripts.
      Garitte, Gérard, "Manuscrits grecs (1940–1950)," *Scriptorium* 6 (1952) 114-46; "Manuscrits grecs (1950–1955)," *Scriptorium* 12 (1958) 118-148. Covers bibliographies, manuals, general treatments, catalogues, history of the Greek manuscript book, notices on various manuscripts.
      Leclerca, Henri, "Manuscrits," *Dictionnaire d'archéologie chrétienne et de liturgie* 10 (1932) 1603-1714.
      Richard, Marcel, *Répertoire des bibliothèques et des catalogues de manuscrits grecs*. 2nd ed. Paris: Centre nationale de recherche scientifique, 1958. A *Supplément* of 78 pp. was published in 1964.
  B. Technical works with reproductions.
      Bascape, G. C. *Paleografia greca e latina*. Milan: Hoepli, 1940. A translation of E. M. Thompson's *Introduction*, below.
      Cucuel, Charles, *Eléments de paléographie grecque* (based on first edition of Gardthausen, *q.v.*). Paris: Klincksieck, 1891.
      Devreesse, Robert, *Introduction à l'étude des manuscrits grecs*. Paris: Klincksieck, 1954.
      Gardthausen, Viktor, *Griechische Palaeographie*. 2nd ed.; 2 vols. Leipzig: Veit, 1911-13.
      Groningen, Bernard Abraham van, *Short Manual of Greek Palaeography*. 3rd ed. Leiden: Sijthoff, 1967. Very practical.
      Montfaucon, Bernardin de, *Palaeographia graeca*. Paris: Guérin, 1708. A monument of erudition that is still of value on minuscule manuscripts.
      Norsa, Medea, *La scrittura letteraria greca dal secolo IV a. C. al secolo VIII d. C.* Florence: Ariani, 1940.
      Schubart, Wilhelm, *Griechische Palaeographie*. Munich: Beck, 1925. Still valuable as a systematic treatment of the subject; S. was an exceptionally gifted paleographer.
      Thompson, Edward Maunde, *Handbook of Greek and Latin Palaeography*. 3rd ed. London: K. Paul, Trench, & Trübner, 1906.
      ———, *An Introduction to Greek and Latin Palaeography*. Oxford: Clarendon Press, 1912. The leading work on the subject in English.

C. Lists: The best lists of the papyri and Greek manuscripts, with date, library, and content, are to be found in:

Aland, Kurt, *Synopsis of the Four Gospels: Greek-English Edition of the Synopsis Quattuor Evangeliorum.* Stuttgart: United Bible Societies, 1972.

————, *Kurzgefasste Liste der griechischen Handschriften des Neuen Testamentes.* Berlin: De Gruyter, 1963.

————, *Studien zur Überlieferung des Neuen Testaments und seines Textes.* Arbeiten zur neutestamentlichen Textforschung 2. Berlin: De Gruyter, 1967.

II. *Special Bibliography*

A. Codex Vaticanus

Codex Vaticanus: Novum Testamentum. 2 vols. Rome, 1881.

Studies. W. H. P. Hatch, *The Principal Uncial Manuscripts of the New Testament* (Chicago: Chicago University Press, 1939); idem, summary of paper on "The Provenance of Codex Vaticanus," in *Journal of Biblical Literature* 72 (1953) xviii-xix; E. Tisserant, "Notes sur la préparation de l'édition en fac-simile typographique du Codex Vaticanus B," *Angelicum* 20 (1943) 237-48.

B. Codex Sinaiticus

Codex Sinaiticus Petropolitanus: e tenebris protaxit Lobegott Frederic Constantinus Tischendorf. St. Petersburg, 1862. A four-volume transcription.

Codex Sinaiticus: Novum Testamentum. Photographic reproduction by Kirsopp and Helen Lake. London, 1911.

Appendix codicum celeberrimorum Sinaitici, Vaticani, Alexandrini cum imitatione ipsorum manu scriptorum, edited by L. F. K. Tischendorf. Leipzig, 1867.

Studies: N. N. Benechevich, *Les manuscrits grecs du Mont Sinaï et le monde savant de l'Europe depuis le XVIIe siècle jusqu'à 1927* (Athens: Verlag der Byzantinisch-neugriechischen Jahrbücher, 1937); G. Garitte, "Expédition paléographique au Sinaî," *Muséon* 63 (1950) 119-21; W. Hotzelt, "La découverte et la vente du codex Sinaiticus," *Theologische Literaturzeitung* 74 (1949) 457-70; J. Johnson, *The Mount Sinai Manuscript of the British Museum* (2nd ed.; Oxford: Trustees of the British Museum, 1934); M.-J. Lagrange, "L'origine médiate et immédiate du manuscrit sinaîtique," *Revue biblique* 35 (1926) 91-92; E. Lauch, "Nichts gegen Tischendorf," in *Bekenntnis zur Kirche: Festgabe für Ernst Sommerlath* (Berlin: Evangelische Verlagsanstalt, 1960), pp. 15-24; H. J. M. Milne and T. C. Skeat, *Scribes and Correctors of the Codex Sinaiticus* (London: British Museum, 1938); O. Schlisske, *De Schatz in Wüstenkloster: Die abenteuerliche Entdeckung der ältesten Bibelhandschrift durch C. von Tischendorf* (Stuttgart: Kreuz-Verlag, 1957); I. Sevcenko, "New Documents on C. Tischendorf and the Codex Sinaiticus," *Scriptorium* 18 (1964) 55-80; C. Tindall, *Contribution to the Statistical Study of the Codex Sinaiticus* (ed. by T. B. Smith, with appendix by A. Q. Morton; Edinburgh: Oliver and Boyd, 1961); L. F. K. Tischendorf, *Mémoire sur la découverte et l'antiquité du codex Sinaiticus* (London: J. E. Taylor, 1865); idem, *Codex Sinaiticus: The Ancient Biblical Manuscript in the British Museum* (8th ed.; London: Lutterworth, 1934).

C. Codex Ephraemi Rescriptus

Ephraemi Syri opera omnia quae exstant, ed. by Joseph Assemani, 6 vols. Rome: Salvioni, 1796. Cf. vol. 4, pp. 144-45.

Codex Ephraemi Rescriptus sive fragments novi Testamenti e codice graeco-parisiensi celeberrimo, ed. by L. F. K. Tischendorf. Leipzig: Tauchnitz, 1843–45. 44 pages of Prolegomena give the place of copying, age of the codex, and remarks on the writing and the correctors.

Fragmenta sacra palimpsesta sive fragmenta cum novi tum veteris Testamenti ex quinque codicibus graecis palimpsestis antiquissimis, edited by L. F. K. Tischendorf. 6 vols. Leipzig: Hinrichs, 1855–69.

Studies: C. R. Gregory, *Bibliotheca Sacra* 33 (1976) 153-93 (biographical article on Tischendorf); R. W. Lyon, "A Re-examination of Codex Ephraemi Rescriptus," *New Testament Studies* 5 (1958–59) 266-72.

D. Codex Alexandrinus

Codex Alexandrinus. 6 vols. London, 1816–28.

Codex Alexandrinus (reduced photographic facsimile). London: British Museum, 1909.

Studies: H. J. M. Milne and T. C. Skeat, *The Codex Sinaiticus and the Codex Alexandrinus* (2nd ed.; Oxford: Oxford University Press, 1955); T. C. Skeat, "The Provenance of the Codex Alexandrinus," *Journal of Theological Studies*, new series, 6 (1955) 233-35.

E. Codex Bezae

Bezae Codex Cantabrigensis. An exact copy in ordinary type, edited with a critical introduction and annotations by A. Scrivener. Cambridge, 1864.

Codex Bezae Cantabrigensis quattuor Evangelia et Actus Apostolorum complectens. Cambridge: Clay, 1890.

Studies: J. R. Harris, *Codex Bezae: A Study of the So-Called Western Text of the New Testament* (Cambridge, 1891); D. H. Quentin, *Le Codex Bezae à Lyon au IXe siècle* (Bruges, 1906); R. C. Stone, *The Language of the Latin Text of Codex Bezae* (Urbana: University of Illinois Press, 1946); H. J. Vogels, *Die Harmonistik im Evangelientext des Codex Cantabrigensis: Ein Beitrag zur neutestamentlichen Textkritik* (Leipzig: Hinrichs, 1910); J. D. Yoder, *Concordance to the Distinctive Greek Text of Codex Bezae* (New Testament Tools and Studies 2; Grand Rapids: Eerdmans, 1961).

F. Codex Freer

Facsimile of the Washington Manuscript of the Four Gospels in the Freer Collection, edited by Henry Arthur Sanders. Michigan, 1912.

Studies: B. Botte, "Freer (Manuscrits de la Collection)," *Dictionnaire de la Bible: Supplément* 3 (1938) 527-30; F. C. Burkitt, "W and Theta Mss.: Studies in the Western Text of Mark," *Journal of Theological Studies* 17 (1915–16) 1-21, 139-52; E. J. Goodspeed, complete collation of Freer W in *American Journal of Theology* 17 (1913) 240-49, 395-411, 599-613; 18 (1914) 131-46, 266-81; E. Jacquier, "La manuscrit Washington des Evangiles," *Revue biblique* 10 (1913) 547-55; idem, *Etudes de critique et de philologie du Nouveau Testament* (Paris, 1920); pp. 486-94; H. A. Sanders, *The New Testament Manuscripts in the Freer Collection* (New York: Macmillan, 1918); A. Souter, "The Freer Washington Ms of the Gospels," *Expositor*, 1914, 350-67; B. H. Streeter, in *Harvard Theological Review* 19 (1926) 165-72 (a ms of the western text, copied at Rome, taken to Caesarea and from there to Alexandria, and corrected in both cities to accord with a local text).

G. Codex Koridethi

Die Koridethi-Evangelia, edited by G. Beermann and C. R. Gregory. Leipzig, 1913.

Studies: B. Botte, "Koridethi (Evangiles de)," *Dictionnaire de la Bible: Supplément* 5 (1957) 192-96; F. C. Burkitt, "The Caesarean Text," *Journal of Theological Studies* 30 (1929) 347-56; M.-J. Lagrange, "Le groupe dit césaréen des Mss des evangiles," *Revue biblique* 38 (1929) 481-512; K. Lake and P. Blake, in *Harvard Theological Review* 16 (1923) 267-86; H. Omont, *Facsimilés des plus anciens mss grecs en onciale et en minuscule du IXe au XIIe siècle* (Paris, 1892); H. J. Vogels, *Codicum Novi Testamenti Specimina* (Bonn, 1929).

Chapter Three

The Minuscule Manuscripts of the Ninth to the Sixteenth Centuries

1. The Minuscule Manuscripts

A new kind of handwriting, called "minuscule," made its appearance in the eighth century, first in private documents in Egypt (Aphroditopolis papyri, 705 A.D.), then in books where it replaced the older writing. It resembles pretty much the writing used for Greek today. Even a quick glance at a page immediately shows the difference between minuscule and majuscule; in minuscule some letters extend above or below the others. Minuscule began as a writing employed in libraries, then came into common use; it later received a fixed form through printing, at which time majuscule supplied the necessary capital letters.

From the eighth to the sixteenth centuries, when the first printed text of the New Testament appeared, 2754 minuscule manuscripts have survived, without counting the 1838 eastern lectionaries for liturgical use. (Uncial or majuscule writing continued in use even after minuscule made its appearance.)

The Uspenskij Evangeliary (Leningrad) dates from 835 and is the oldest dated minuscule manuscript we have. As time went on, minuscule writing developed and gradually replaced uncial, which however continued to be used for some centuries in the form of liturgical uncial.

The reproduction in plate 46 of six verses (John 17:7-12) in the Uspenskij Evangeliary, now in the State Library at Leningrad, shows us the neat writing of the monk Nikolai, who has signed and dated his manuscript. The photograph is from Th. L. Lefort's *Album Palaeographicum* which contains ninety reproductions of manuscripts dating from the ninth and tenth centuries.

The manuscript was almost certainly written at the monastery of Studios in Constantinople. It shows all the characteristics of the oldest minuscule, the so-called pure minuscule: there is no admixture of un-

33

cials except at the end of lines; the letters are equal in height and uniform; some are connected with others according to set rules; sometimes letters are united by ligatures in which a part of each letter fuses with the other letter, but never to the point of deforming the letter. There is no separation of words, since the only divisions derive from the rules for ligature proper to each letter. Moreover, every letter that can be joined to the following letter is in fact habitually joined to it.

The breathing marks are squarish, the accents small and clear; abbreviations are few and are, for practical purposes, limited to contractions of the "sacred names." The letter *n* is omitted at the end of a line; conventional signs replace the endings of the declensions and the coordinating conjunction "and."

2. CODEX 70 OF PARIS

Greek codex 70 of Paris is written on vellum and contains the four Gospels. Each Gospel is preceded by a painting that shows grace and refinement (cf. pl. 48).

This codex of 392 pages was part of Cardinal Mazarin's library. Despite a notation by a later hand, it does not date from before the end of the ninth century; the writing is the consciously refined, even mannered writing that is found only beginning in the early years of the tenth century. The book was probably written for an important library or personage and belongs among the early Greek minuscules that range from the first quarter of the tenth century to the last quarter of the eleventh.

3. CODEX 89 OF PARIS

The Paris Greek manuscript 89 also contains the four Gospels and belongs to the Bibliothèque de Colbert. It has a few marginal annotations.

It contains 169 pages, of which only one, page 158, is mutilated. It was written in the twelfth century in a straightforward, clear, practiced hand resembling that of contemporary texts of Aeschylus and Sophocles.

A completely pure minuscule did not last very long; gradually, such uncial letters as had specifically minuscule forms began to be used as well. By the end of the tenth century all the uncial and minuscule forms are interchangeable, although we do not necessarily find the use of all the forms side by side in every manuscript. The reader may verify what we have been saying by studying plates 52 and 53 with a good magnifying glass.

The final pages of this manuscript list the sections of the Gospel recited in the Greek Office each day.

4. CODEX 74 OF PARIS

Greek manuscript 74 in the National Library at Paris contains 215 pages and is written on paper made from cotton in the twelfth century. Ligatures are numerous; every line has some uncial letters; the breathing marks have an angular shape; a † sign precedes words spoken by Jesus. What renders this codex especially attractive is the rather tasteful illustrations scattered through its pages; plates 54 and 56 offer some excellent examples. The codex used to be part of the Médicis collection at Paris.

We need not give details of further minuscule manuscripts. The great majority of minuscules have little value when it comes to establishing the text of the New Testament. The exceptions are those minuscule manuscripts which are copies of valuable majuscules or uncial manuscripts that have been lost but are known to have existed.

There is work, here, then for the philologist who is dealing with the biblical text. Since we have the amateur in view, it would be useless to give more examples, but we must at least note that the work of the biblical paleographer is being immensely facilitated by photography.

The extensive development of the American university faculties that are occupied with biblical texts and ancient texts generally is due to the fact that hundreds of kilometers of microfilm are now at the disposal of scholars. 900 km of microfilm were taken at the Vatican in 1950, and 50 km more at Mount Sinai in 1960. All these manuscripts can be read with as much ease as if the student had the original in front of him; they can be scrutinized even more closely than the originals as far as the essentials go.

Papyri may be yellowish, darkened, and dirty; when photographed, the background emerges as white, so that the color of the ink stands out. Evidently, then, we can expect splendid reproductions from a good team of photographers. If the reader could see how dark brown John Rylands Papyrus 457 is, he would be amazed at the clarity of our plates 2 and 4 where only the ink shows up.

If a complete collation of all the New Testament papyri and manuscripts were to be made, we would have a text almost identical with the one written between 52 and 95 A.D.

Bibliography on the Minuscule Manuscripts

Colwell, Ernest Cadman, "Method in Locating a Newly Discovered Manuscript within the Manuscript Tradition of the New Testament," in *Studia Evangelica* 1. Texte and Untersuchungen 73. Berlin: Akademie-Verlag, 1959. Pp. 757–77.

Hatch, William Henry, *Facsimiles and Descriptions of Minuscule Manuscripts of the New Testament.* Cambridge, Mass., 1951. An important work, containing 100 reproductions, and studies of writing and the history of the text.

Lake, Kirsopp and Silva, *Dated Greek Minuscule Manuscripts to the Year 1200.* 2 vols., 800 plates. Boston, 1934–45. A mine of documents drawn from all libraries.

Metzger, Bruce M., *The Text of the New Testament: Its Transmission, Corruption and Restoration.* New York: Oxford University Press, 1964. Pp. 61–67.

Turyn, Alexander, *Codices graeci vaticani (1203–1394).* Vatican City, 1964.

Wikenhauser, Alfred, *New Testament Introduction*, tr. by Joseph Cunningham. New York: Herder and Herder, 1958. Pp. 78–90.

Chapter Four

The New Testament after the Introduction of Printing

1. Sixteenth to Eighteenth Centuries

As early as 1500 publishers were thinking of an edition of the New Testament in Greek. Between 1450 and 1456 St. Jerome's Latin Vulgate had been printed by Gutenberg at Mainz, and before 1500 bibles had been issued in Czech, French, German, and Italian.

Although the first Greek grammar was published in Milan in 1476, it was not until 1516 that a complete edition of the New Testament saw the light. The reason for the delay was that the interested parties wanted to imitate in print the decorative minuscule writing of the fifteenth century with its ligatures of two and even three letters. The results can be seen in the specimens of Erasmus' edition and of the Alcalá Bible (plates 58 and 60).

The honor of having sponsored the first Greek edition of the Bible belongs to Francisco Ximénez de Cisneros, Cardinal Archbishop of Toledo. In 1502 he undertook the preparation of a polyglot bible with parallel columns giving the Hebrew, Aramaic (in some books), Greek, and Latin texts; the whole was to be in six large folio volumes.

The original edition comprised six hundred copies, of which ninety-seven are known today (according to James P. R. Lyell, *Cardinal Ximénez*, London, 1917). The university town of Alcalá (Latin: Complutum) gave the book its name, *Complutensis Biblia*. Volume 5, containing the New Testament and a Greek-Latin vocabulary, was published, according to its colophon, on January 10, 1514. Volume 6, with appendixes, a Hebrew lexicon, and a Hebrew grammar, came from the presses in 1515, while the four volumes of the Old Testament were issued on July 10, 1517.

The approbation of Pope Leo X, which is printed in volume 1, was obtained only on March 22, 1520, when the manuscripts borrowed from the Vatican Library were returned. The Polyglot of Alcalá seems to have gotten into circulation, however, only in 1522.

Scholars have not been able to decide just which manuscript served as the basis for the Alcalá text; cf. Franz Delitzsch's *Studies on the Complutensian Polyglot* (London, 1872). The first Greek New Testament that actually reached the marketplace was that of Desiderius Erasmus of Rotterdam (1469–1536). It is too bad that it did.

When did Erasmus first decide to bring out his edition? No one knows for sure. During a visit to Basel in August 1514 he discussed the possibility of such an edition with Johann Froben, the publisher. No further steps were taken until April, 1515, when Forben, who had heard of the Alcalá polyglot, offered Erasmus any sum he might name for an edition.

In July, 1515, Erasmus went to Basel hoping to find Greek manuscripts he might publish along with the Latin translation he had been working on for seven years. He himself had only two manuscripts, of mediocre value and incomplete. Erasmus looked on this as a challenge, and, since the last page of the Apocalypse was missing, he made a Greek translation from his own Latin to take its place. Then, in record time, his Greek and Latin New Testament was issued on March 1, 1516. The Greek text was of only average value, and the book was full of typographical errors.

We can see, then, how the "received text" of the Greek New Testament came to have its dominant position until the end of the nineteenth century. In three years Froben sold over three thousand copies of his edition; he had won the battle against Alcalá. Despite the critical reaction of Cambridge and Oxford, this text spread across Europe, even though it represented only a half-dozen incomplete minuscule manuscripts of the twelfth century. Thanks to a Latin translation that Erasmus had revised, a Greek text of little critical value dominated the market for four hundred years.

The Alcalá Bible was marked by fine textual criticism, but only six hundred copies of it appeared, in 1522, and so it exercised little influence. Commercial competitiveness is not a twentieth-century invention; Froben is a good example of it four centuries ago.

The first edition of the whole Bible in Greek was published in February 1518 by the famous Aldine press at Venice. The New Testament part follows Erasmus' text so closely as to reproduce even the typographical errors that Erasmus corrected in his errata.

The well-known publisher and printer, Robert Estienne (Stephanus) of Paris (1503–59) published four editions of the Bible in Greek, three at Paris and the fourth at Geneva in 1551. The third, folio edition is the first New Testament to have a critical apparatus. Here for the first time the Bible was also divided into numbered verses. It has been said jokingly that this division was made by Estienne as he traveled on horseback from Lyons to Paris; more likely he did it while resting at the various inns.

The division of the Bible into chapters is older, but not ancient. It has been attributed to Stephen Langton (1150–1228), archbishop of Canterbury, but was more probably the work of Hugo Cardinalis (1200–1263), who edited the first concordance of biblical texts. In any case, the chapter divisions hardly follow any valid logic.

Theodore of Beza (1519–1605), friend and successor of Calvin at Geneva, and an eminent biblical scholar, published no less than nine editions of the Greek Bible from 1565 to 1604. He himself collated a number of Greek manuscripts; he also had in his possession the codex named after him, Codex Bezae, but did not make any great use of it. What he really did was to popularize and stereotype the "received text" which then served as the working text for the English translators of the King James Bible (1611). Beza was more of a theologian than a text critic; he did not grasp the importance of a correct text and kept few readings of his own.

In 1624, the brothers Bonaventure and Abraham Elzevier, enterprising publishers at Leiden in Holland, printed a small-format, practical edition of the Greek New Testament; the text is that of Beza's edition of 1565. *Textus receptus sed non recipiendus* (a text received that should not be received): the Greek text which everyone accepted but which did not deserve anyone's confidence nonetheless became the "received" text. Its "reception," however, was effected by booksellers' advertising. No new scientific method for getting at the original had been applied, and the text was simply a reproduction of Beza's first edition. The Elzevier brothers did, however, do a very careful printing job, and produced a handy pocket edition at a reasonable price.

The domination of the "received" text lasted from 1633 to 1831 in England, as far as the work of spreading the Bible was concerned; even the British and Foreign Bible Society accepted it. Meanwhile, however, the philologists continued their work at Cambridge and Oxford, although their immense labor had hardly any influence on the text of successive new editions.

France had lost its opportunity to take the lead in textual criticism of the Bible. Toward the end of the seventeenth century Richard Simon (1638–1712) had begun the task of putting textual criticism on a scientific basis, but he worked in isolation. His four monumental publications might have started a type of biblical research that would have been well ahead of what the universities of the day were doing. His books were: *L'histoire critique du texte du Nouveau Testament* (Rotterdam, 1689); *L'histoire critique des versions du Nouveau Testament* (Rotterdam, 1690); *L'histoire critique des principaux commentateurs du Nouveau Testament* (2 vols.; Rotterdam, 1693); *Nouvelles observations sur le texte et les versions du Nouveau Testament* (Paris, 1695).

Simon did not start with the traditional, dogmatic presuppositions of his age but approached the text of the Bible critically, as a work of literature. He had already glimpsed what would be critically valid in the modern *formgeschichtlich* (history of forms) approach, and his works are full of accurate observations. He was two or three centuries ahead of his time in dealing with details, and anticipated the conclusions reached by modern scholarship.

The first serious attack on the received text came from Richard Bentley (1662–1742), who was already famous at Cambridge for his critical edition of Horace and for the discovery of the digamma in the poems of Homer. Bentley believed that by following the earliest manuscripts he could restore the New Testament to the state it had in the fourth century, but he died before carrying out his plan.

With Johann Albrecht Bengel (1687–1752) we reach a new stage in the history of New Testament text criticism. Bengel's 1734 edition (at Tübingen) probably seems unduly timid, but the critical apparatus lists new variants even when the received text is kept, as it usually is. In the critical apparatus at the end of the work Bengel gives a scientific foundation for his classification of variants, grouping the manuscripts into families on the basis of the readings they show. The details of the classification are open to argument at times, but the principle underlying it is a credit to Bengel. Despite his well-known personal piety and the fact that he was pastor of the Evangelical church at Württemberg, his own people regarded him as an enemy of the sacred Scriptures, and he was obliged to write a defense of the New Testament in order to explain his purposes and his edition.

Among Bengel's helpers was Johann Jakob Wettstein (1693–1754), a native of Basel. His penchant for textual criticism showed itself quite early, but his studies were interpreted as preparation on his part for a denial of the divinity of Christ, and in 1730 he was forced to give up his pastorate. He became professor of Hebrew at Amsterdam, and in 1752 his forty years of study bore fruit in the publication at Amsterdam of his magnificent two-volume folio edition of the New Testament (reprinted by photo-offset in 1967). The text is simply that of the Elzevier brothers, but it is accompanied by an extensive criticial apparatus, all the fuller since the entries take up less space thanks to an ingenious system of signs.

2. THE MODERN PERIOD

In the last half of the eighteenth century the German scholar Johann Jakob Griesbach (1745–1812) laid the foundations for all later work on the Greek text of the New Testament. He was professor at the University of Jena from 1775 until his death; he traveled to England, Holland, and France to collate manuscripts, especially the Gothic, Armenian, and Syriac versions.

Griesbach did a great deal of research into the history of the transmission of the New Testament text in the early centuries, and on the basis of it divided all recensions into three groups: the Alexandrian, the Western, and the Byzantine. It would be difficult to overestimate Griesbach's importance in the field of text criticism; he showed great ability and judgment in weighing the value of different readings. For example, his judgment, based on the Fathers and the versions, that the short form is to be preferred in the Lord's Prayer (Luke 9:3-4), was remarkably confirmed when the readings of Codex Vaticanus were published, since all of his omissions were supported by this ancient manuscript. For the first time, moreover, a German scholar dared abandon at many points the text that had been "received" since Erasmus' time.

In his editions of the Greek New Testament: Halle, 1774–77; Jena, 1796–1806, and Leipzig, 1807 (representing his definitive judgment), he deserves to be regarded as a real pioneer in text criticism. Others in Germany followed his example. The collections of variants, their methodical classification according to families of manuscripts, and the critical hypotheses concerning these documents were all a preparation for the next period.

3. THE REJECTION OF THE "RECEIVED" TEXT

The first scholar to make a sharp break with the "received" text was Karl Lachmann of Berlin (1793–1851), a philologist at home both in the classical and the Germanic languages. He is well-known for his editions of Catullus, Tibullus, and Lucretius, and the *Nibelungenlied*.

As far as the New Testament is concerned his aim was to recover the text that was current in eastern Christendom at the end of the fourth century. This famous philologist did valuable pioneer work, but he tended to forget that in the New Testament manuscripts, more than in the works of classical literature, there are deliberate variants. As a result he did not allow sufficient scope for internal criticism.

Lobegott Friedrich Konstantin von Tischendorf (1815–74) is the individual to whom modern New Testament criticism is most indebted, not only for his discovery and publication of manuscripts but also for his eight editions of the Greek Bible. He traveled throughout Europe and the East in search of new manuscripts; he discovered twenty uncial manuscripts (eighteen of them very valuable) and collated the variants of twenty-three.

The last edition of his Greek New Testament in 1872 (*editio octava critica maior*; cf. plate 62) abandoned the "received" text which he had been following since 1841. Tischendorf now changed his whole approach and followed closely the text of the Codex Sinaiticus which he had published in 1862. According to Eberhard Nestle, the eighth edition differs from the seventh in 3572 places.

The critical apparatus of this eighth edition (the only edition scholars have in mind when they speak of Tischendorf's New Testament) is still an indispensable working-tool; nothing as complete exists elsewhere, especially for citations from the Fathers. Tischendorf's text itself is in fact much less important. In the last analysis the scholarly professor from Leipzig was not guided by any firm principle. He was an enthusiastic and lucky researcher, an active and alert editor, and a fervent collector of variants, but he did not have a critical mind in the strict sense of the term. In general, he was in the Lachmann tradition, preferring the oldest Greek texts.

He did not have time to publish the Prolegomena to his work. This part, a real summa of textual criticism, we owe to one of his disciples, Caspar-René Gregory, who published it at Leipzig, 1884–94, and then brought out a corrected and enlarged version of it, under the title *Textkritik des Neuen Testaments* (3 vols.; Lepizig, 1900–1909).

To sum up: Tischendorf does not represent a real advance in the methods of New Testament text criticism but rather used those of his predecessors a little more flexibly, while leaving room for internal criticism to play its part. His chief claim to fame is as discoverer and editor of new witnesses to the text. He was a learned man, at home with variants. On the whole, his work is a monument to solid foundations, but it is lacking in finesse.

The year 1881 brought the publication of the most solid critical edition of the New Testament ever produced by British scholars. In that year, Brooke Foss Westcott (1825–1901) and Fenton John Anthony Hort (1828–1898), professors at Cambridge, published *The New Testament in the Original Greek*, the fruit of thirty years of collaboration. Volume 1 contained the text, with the variants in the margin, and a short explanation of the method followed. Volume 2, the work of Hort, contained an introduction to New Testament text criticism and an appendix which gives a detailed commentary on the readings that were rejected.

The work of these two scholars is based on a careful examination of the variants, and their originality consists in the progress they represent in the methods of text criticism, since they succeeded in properly evaluating the mass of documents which Tischendorf had gathered.

On the basis of their study of the witnesses to the text, they distinguish four main types of text: the Syrian, best represented by the Codex Alexandrinus; the Western, preserved in the Codex Bezae; the Alexandrine, found in the Codex Ephraemi and the Coptic versions; and the Neutral, represented by Codex Vaticanus and Codex Sinaiticus.

The title of Westcott and Hort's work voices a hope that has not been fulfilled: to restore perfectly the original Greek text of the New Testament. This the scholars have not yet succeeded in doing. They have not yet made full use of all the manuscripts available, but Westcott and Hort do represent an important advance.

4. The Work of Hermann von Soden (1852–1914)

By far the most monumental edition of the New Testament

produced in the twentieth century is that of Hermann Freiherr von Soden, born in Cincinnati and killed in an accident on the Berlin subway in 1914.

With the financial help of Elise Koenigs, von Soden was able to send a large number of students and scholars to the libraries of Europe and the Near East. But, despite this and other advantages von Soden enjoyed, his work was not a complete success, for he had hoped to introduce a new nomenclature, and this in turn made necessary the construction of a new key, such as we have in Friedrich Krüger's *Schlüssel zu von Sodens Die Schriften des Neuen Testaments* (Göttingen, 1927).

Five editions produced in the twentieth century are excellent for study purposes: those of Heinrich Joseph Vogels (Düsseldorf, 1920); Augustin Merk (Rome, 1933); José María Bover (Madrid, 1943); G. D., Kilpatrick (London, 1958); Erwin Nestle and Kurt Aland (Stuttgart, 1963).

From 1922 to 1930 eight congresses were held under the auspices of the Church History Society (*Gesellschaft für Kirchengeschichte*) of Germany. The aim was to unify the work being done on New Testament text criticism, but what emerged was an irreconcilable opposition between the British and the Germans with regard to a new edition of Tischendorf. The British wanted to retain as a basis the text that had been "received" since the beginning of the seventeenth century, while the German's wanted to use von Soden's edition though it was somewhat marred by oversystematization.

In 1948 the International Greek New Testament Project was begun. It enlisted the scholars of Great Britain and the United States in an effort to establish a valid critical apparatus for the Greek New Testament. The work is still going on.

In May, 1946, the British and Foreign Bible Society decided to embark on a new translation of the Bible. The New Testament part was published in 1961 by the Oxford and Cambridge University Presses. In 1967 it was also issued on records that are technically far superior to Deiss' recordings of the four Gospels in French. The Greek text on which the New English Bible is based was edited by R. V. G. Tasker in 1964; it is a handsome book, but does not represent a real advance in textual criticism.

Finally, the Württembergische Bibelanstalt at Stuttgart has published two remarkable examples of textual criticism. One is Kurt Aland's *Synopsis quattuor Evangeliorum locis parallelis evangeliorum apocryphorum* (7th ed., 1971). With its critical apparatus this makes an excellent tool for work on the New Testament. [The *Synopsis of the Four Gospels: Greek-English Edition of the Synopsis quattuor Evangeliorum* (1972) has the full apparatus but lacks the parallels from apocryphal gospels and patristic sources.]

The other is *The Greek New Testament*, edited by Kurt Aland (Münster), Matthew Black (Saint Andrews), Bruce M. Metzger (Princeton), and Allen Wikgren (Chicago) (2nd ed., 1968). This first-rate critical edition is an important step toward the restoration of the original text of the New Testament, an important step in the process we have been following through the centuries beginning with Manchester Papyrus 457, that is, with the years between 100 and 120 A.D.

Bibliography on Editions of the Greek New Testament

I. *Editions*
  A. Catalogue
    Darlow, T. H., and H. F. Moule, *Historical Catalogue of the Printed Editions of the Holy Scripture*. 5 vols. London: British and Foreign Bible Society, 1963. Cf. vol., 2, pp. 573–678.
  B. Editions (in chronological order according to date of first edition)
    Desiderius Erasmus, *Novum Testamentum Graece*. Basel, 1516.
    Complutensis Biblia ("Polyglot of Alcalá"). Printed in six vols., 1514–17, but not published until 1522.
    Robert Estienne (Stephanus), *Biblia*, Paris, 1546. The best known edition is the third, the *Editio regia*, of 1550.
    Theodore of Beza, *Novum Testamentum cujus graeco contextui respondent interpretationes duae, una vetus, altera Theodori*. Paris, 1565.
    Wettstein, Johann Jakob, *Novum Testamentum Graecum*. Graz, 1752. Photomechanical reprint, 1962.
    Tischendorf, L. F. K. von, *Novum Testamentum Graecum*. Leipzig, 1841. *Editio octava critica maior*, 2 vols.; Leipzig, 1869–72.
    Westcott, Brooke Foss, and Fenton John Anthony Hort, *The New Testament in the Original Greek*. Cambridge, 1881.
    Nestle, Eberhard, *Novum Testamentum Graece*. Stuttgart, 1898. 25th edition by Erwin Nestle and Kurt Aland, Stuttgart, 1963.
    Souter, Alexander, *Novum Testamentum Graece*. Oxford, 1910. 2nd edition, 1947.
    Soden, Hermann von, *Die Schriften des Neuen Testamentes in ihrer ältesten erreichbaren Textgestalt*. 4 vols.; Göttingen, 1902–13.
    Vogels, Heinrich Joseph, *Novum Testamentum Graece et Latine*. Düsseldorf, 1920. 3rd edition, Freiburg, 1950.
    Merk, Augustin, *Novum Testamentum Graece et Latine*. Rome, 1933. 8th edition by S. Lyonnet, 1957.
II. Some Readings
    Armstrong, Elizabeth, *Robert Estienne, Royal Printer: An Historical Study of the Elder Stephanus*. Cambridge: Cambridge University Press, 1954.
    Coppens, Joseph, "Erasme, exégète et théologien," *Ephemerides Theologicae Lovanienses* 44 (1968) 191–204.
    Erasmus: Catalogue de l'exposition au Musée Boymans à Rotterdam. Anderlecht-Brussels, 19
    Margolin, J. C., *Erasmus par lui-même*. Paris: Editions du Seuil, 1965.
    Steinmann, Jean, *Richard Simon et les origines de l'exégèse biblique*. Paris: Editions du Cerf, 1960.
III. Reference Works
    Dictionnaire de la Bible: Supplément, begun by L. Pirot, continued by H. Cazelles and A. Feuillet. Paris, 1928 — Synthetic studies of the Bible and the civilizations of the biblical east.
    Duplacy, Jean, "Bulletin de critique textuelle du Nouveau Testament," *Recherches de science religieuse* 45 (1957) 419–41; 46 (1958) 270–313, 431–62; 50 (1962) 242–63, 564–98; 51 (1963) 432–62; 53 (1965) 257–84; 54 (1966) 426–76.
    Theologisches Wörterbuch zum Neuen Testament, begun by Gerhard Kittel, continued by Gerhard Friedrich. 9 vols.; Stuttgart, 1933–73. English edition by Geoffrey W. Bromiley, *Theological Dictionary of the New Testament*. 9 vols.; Grand Rapids, 1964–74.

Conclusion

This essay has taken us from the generation which saw the appearance of the Fourth Gospel down to the most recent contributions to the establishment of a critical text.

What an abyss of time separates the first known manuscripts of the classical Greek authors from the originals! Fourteen centuries for Sophocles and Aeschylus, sixteen for Plato, twelve for Demosthenes. And yet for the Gospel of St. John an uninterrupted chain of witnesses takes us back from the sixteenth century to the great manuscripts of the first half of the fourth century and the papyri of the second century. This chain gives us complete historical certainty about the New Testament, the composition of which took from about 51 A.D. (Letters to the Thessalonians) to the last decade of the first century (Gospel of St. John).

The manuscript tradition is an external critical argument for the existence of the text of the Fourth Gospel from about the year 100. It is impossible for anyone in good faith to assign the composition of this Gospel to a date much later than the last decade of the first century. This fact is important for philology and exegesis.

We have cast a rapid glance at the huge pile of 2754 minuscule manuscripts written from the ninth to the sixteenth century. We have acted like tourists admiring monuments, but we must not forget that others, very many others, have worked this mine. In any event, those working on the minuscules did not as it were have to discover the basic text; that had been done with aid of the 266 uncial manuscripts and the 81 papyri. The scholars dealing with the minuscules have been performing a task proper to internal criticism: sorting out variants that affect about an eighth of the text.

Evidently, when we deal with a Greek work that exists in only one manuscript, as is the case with Aristotle's *Constitution of Athens*, there is no question of variants; we can only discuss the value of the one text we have. Now, despite the existence of variants, the New Testament, and the Fourth Gospel in particular, are almost identical in the Tischendorf edition of 1872 or the Nestle-Aland edition of 1963 and in the Bodmer Papyrus which gives us the first fourteen chapters of John as they looked about 200 A.D., or Manchester Papyrus 457 which gives us a fragment of John 18 from an even earlier time. Here the reader should look once again at the photographs of the papyri with their transcriptions and compare them with the critical editions of Nestle-Aland (plate 63), Tischendorf (plates 61–62), and Aland-Black-Metzger-Wikgren (plate 65).

He will become convinced that our present text of the Fourth Gospel has incontestable historical value.

There is, of course, the further, supremely important question of the historicity of the Gospel's content. It is not our purpose in this essay to face this question. We simply refer the reader to two experts in this area. One is Charles H. Dodd, Cambridge professor, who died in 1965. By way of conclusion to his *Historical Tradition in the Fourth Gospel* (Cambridge: Cambridge University Press, 1963), he writes:

> Behind the Fourth Gospel lies an ancient tradition independent of the other gospels, and meriting serious consideration as a contribution to our knowledge of the historical facts concerning Jesus Christ (p. 423).
> To reach some measure of objective historical judgement (relatively objective, as all such judgements must be), the tradition, envisaged as clearly as may be, must be set firmly in its total historical environment, by the use of all available evidence. Our knowledge of this environment — of outward conditions and of what was in the minds of men — is in our time receiving welcome increment, both from freshly discovered material and from the intensive study of the period from many points of view. The enterprise of working towards a clear and well-based conception of the historical facts upon which our religion is founded is a promising one, and the mood of defeatism which for some time prevailed is rightly beginning to give way to a more hopeful resumption of the "quest of the historical Jesus" (p. 432).

The second expert, Béda Rigaux, sums up the state of the question as follows in a radio talk of June 1965:

Should we regard the Gospels as trustworthy historical documents? The question has elicited quite varying answers from the biblical critics. Eighteenth-century rationalism denied any historical value to the Gospels on the grounds that they were written by men who accepted an outdated supernaturalism. Kantianism and Hegelianism, at the beginning of the nineteenth century explained the Gospels as a movement of thought in which the thesis of Peter and the antithesis of Paul lead to the synthesis of Luke. The liberals at the end of the century allowed Jesus whatever they would within the framework of a philosophy that rejected both miracle and mystery. Those working in the history of religions turned him into a mythological god; others regarded him as the deluded preacher of the end of the world. Finally, in the most recent stage in the development of philosophy, existentialism has thrown history to the winds and opted for a Lutheran faith that has no basis in historical fact.

These divergent views (evidently presented in an extremely simplified form) agree on one point: the Gospels are not to be taken as historical documents, since both reason and science prevent modern man from accepting the Gospel witness as understood by a contemporary reading of the texts.

But, then, what happens to historical research in all of this? Must I abdicate my faith in order to understand the Gospels? Or does my faith rather make it possible for me to understand the assertions made by witnesses to the life of Jesus? Does not the rejection of the supernatural, on the contrary, denature the teaching and actions of Jesus and turn him into a mere moralist, a preacher of love for God and of peace among men? But if this last reading be accepted, how explain the fact that Jesus made so many enemies and that they put him to death? Thus, the critics avoid one riddle only to find themselves confronted with another.

Well, then, they say, it was the enthusiastic faith of the disciples and the early communities that created the Gospel picture of Jesus. But where is such creative power to be found? It is religious geniuses who create; communities merely receive. This supposed explanation thus replaces the Jesus of the Gospels with an anonymous throng of geniuses, no trace of whom has survived, no name to which we can attribute a power we refuse to the one these early Christians acknowledged as their master!

The critics, in a more subtle move, also ask us to elaborate a new concept of history that will embrace the whole of reality, including the supernatural. We are not to distinguish any longer between the adhesion of faith to realities which reason cannot grasp, and the testimony of the sources which require the historian to pass judgment on facts. But here, once again, we must refuse. History cannot force an act of faith upon the believer, but it can and must present all comers with a sum of facts and teachings that confront them with a question: Are we to accept or reject the judgment of the witnesses? History has its own necessary function. It raises the question: Does the apostolic witness concerning Jesus, the Jesus of history, deserve our credence?

Even the most radical of the critics today admit, in virtue of this testimony, that Jesus existed, that he preached the coming of God's reign, that he broke with his people on essential points of their belief, such as the value of the sabbath, the place of the law, ritual cleanness and uncleanness, divorce, etc. We will even find scholars who have grown weary of philosophical systems and are returning to history, where they reject a scepticism they now regard as outdated.

A new approach to Jesus is being implemented. The study of Jesus' own language, Aramaic, and of the Jewish sources of the time, especially the Qumran documents, is showing us that the words put on Jesus' lips in the Gospels have the Semitic character proper to natives of Palestine.

Moreover, there are sayings in the Gospels which must come from Jesus himself: the invocation of God as "our father," an address unknown in the whole religious literature; the designation of himself as "Son of Man"; the statement, so scandalous to the community, that even the Son did not know the day or hour of the coming of God's reign; the reproach to Peter, treating him as "Satan"; the characteristic formulas, "This is my body," "This is my blood," and many others.

Other words of Jesus that belong to the earliest strata of the Gospels point in the same direction: "Your sins are forgiven you," "The sabbath was made for man, not man for the sabbath," "He who acknowledges me on earth, I will acknowledge in heaven."

Then there are all the difficult sayings that seem to link the present time with the manifestation of the messianic glory: "This generation shall not pass away before all this comes to pass."

We may proceed a step further and ask to whom, if not to the Galilean master, we are to attribute the teaching in parables and the Matthaean antitheses: "Moses said to you . . . but I say to you. . . ." The parables are a new genre that has never been imitated; the antitheses presuppose a claim to authority that the Jews rightly regarded as blasphemous.

Who, moreover, could have imagined a messenger from God who has such intimate dealings with his Father?

In Jesus God fulfills his promises and even goes beyond them. Jesus unites in himself the power of a wonderworker and the weakness of a man who dies with the words on his lips, "Father, why have you abandoned me?" He expels demons and requires figs of a tree which could not supply them at that season; he preaches the most sublime morality men have ever heard: "Be perfect as my Father is perfect," and calls sinners to follow him.

We must ask, then: Does not the Gospel image of Jesus carry with it the proof of its authenticity?

Faith is born of facts, it does not create the facts. It is testimony that enables us to establish the facts, in this case as in any other event of the historical past. We must choose between the *ipse dixits* of the philosophers and the testimony of the apostles and disciples. Like the contemporaries of Jesus we are confronted with the question: Whom do you say that I am? The believer answers: "You are the Christ, the Son of God." This confession of faith has a solid footing in history.

Plate 1 49

1. Hall of the John Rylands Library, Manchester, with the cases containing the papyri. Papyrus 457 is in the second case on the left.

2. Papyrus 457, recto and verso. Only the recto page is visible in the glass-covered case.

Plate 3 51

ΟΙ ΙΟΥΔΑΙΟΙ ΗΜΙ
ΟΥΔΕΝΑ ΙΝΑ Ο Λ
ΠΕΝ ΣΗΜΑΙΝΩ
ΘΝΗΣΚΕΙΝ ΙΣ
ΡΙΟΝ Ο Π
ΚΑΙ ΕΪΠ
ΛΙΩ

οι ιουδαιοι ημι
ουδενα ινα ο λ
πεν σημαινω
θνηϲκειν ιϲ
ριον ο π
και ειπ
αιω

ΥΤΟ ΓΕΓΕΝΝΗΜΑΙ
ΣΜΟΝ ΙΝΑ ΜΑΡΤΥ
ΕΚ ΤΗΣ ΑΛΗΘΕ
ΛΕΓΕΙ ΑΥΤΩ
ΑΙ ΤΟΥΤΟ
ΤΟΥΣ Ι
ΕΜΙ

υτο γεγεννημαι
σμον ινα μαρτυ
εκ της αληθε
λεγει αυτω
αι τουτο
τους ι
εμι

3. Transcription into upper- and lower-case letters of the letters legible on the papyrus.

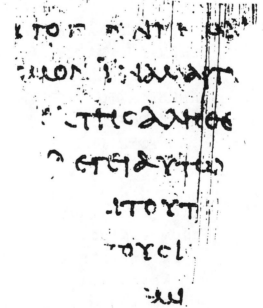

4. A photograph which eliminates the yellow and brownish tones from the papyrus.

Plate 5 53

ΟΙ ΙΟΥΔΑΙΟΙ ΗΜΙΝ ΟΥΚ ΕΞΕΣΤΙΝ ΑΠΟΚΤΕΙΝΑΙ
ΟΥΔΕΝΑ ΙΝΑ Ο ΛΟΓΟΣ ΤΟΥ ΙΗΣΟΥ ΠΛΗΡΩΘΗ ΟΝ ΕΙ
ΠΕΝ ΣΗΜΑΙΝΩΝ ΠΟΙΩ ΘΑΝΑΤΩ ΗΜΕΛΛΕΝ ΑΠΟ
ΘΝΗΣΚΕΙΝ ΙΣΗΛΘΕΝ ΟΥΝ ΠΑΛΙΝ ΕΙΣ ΤΟ ΠΡΑΙΤΩ
ΡΙΟΝ Ο ΠΙΛΑΤΟΣ ΚΑΙ ΕΦΩΝΗΣΕΝ ΤΟΝ ΙΗΣΟΥΝ
ΚΑΙ ΕΙΠΕΝ ΑΥΤΩ ΣΥ ΕΙ Ο ΒΑΣΙΛΕΥΣ ΤΩΝ ΙΟΥ
ΔΑΙΩΝ ΑΠΕΚΡΙΘΗ ΙΗΣΟΥΣ.....

οἱ Ἰουδαῖοι, ʽημῖν οὐκ ἔξεστιν ἀποκτεῖναι.
οὐδενα. ἵνα ὁ λόγος τοῦ Ἰησοῦ πληρωθῇ ὃν εἶ-
-πεν σημαίνων ποίῳ θανάτῳ ἤμελλεν ἀπο-
-θνῇσκειν .Ἰσῆλθεν οὖν πάλιν εἰς το πραιτώ-
-ριον ὁ Πιλᾶτος και ἐφώνησεν. τον Ἰησοῦν
και εἶπεν αὐτῷ , Συ εἶ ὁ βασιλευς τῶν Ἰου-
-δαίων ; ἀπεκρίθη Ἰησοῦς ....

       ΣΥ ΛΕΓΕΙΣ ΟΤΙ ΒΑΣΙ
ΛΕΥΣ ΕΙΜΙ ΕΓΩ ΕΙΣ ΤΟΥΤΟ ΓΕΓΕΝΝΗΜΑΙ
ΚΑΙ ΕΙΣ ΤΟΥΤΟΕΛΗΛΥΘΑ ΕΙΣ ΤΟΝ ΚΟΣΜΟΝ ΙΝΑ ΜΑΡΤΥ
ΡΗΣΩ ΤΗ ΑΛΗΘΕΙΑ ΠΑΣ Ο ΩΝ ΕΚ ΤΗΣ ΑΛΗΘΕΙΑΣ
ΑΚΟΥΕΙ ΜΟΥ ΤΗΣ ΦΩΝΗΣ ΛΕΓΕΙ ΑΥΤΩ
Ο ΠΙΛΑΤΟΣ ΤΙ ΕΣΤΙΝ ΑΛΗΘΕΙΑ. ΚΑΙ ΤΟΥΤΟ
ΕΙΠΩΝ ΠΑΛΙΝ ΕΞΗΛΘΕΝ ΠΡΟΣ ΤΟΥΣ ΙΟΥ
ΔΑΙΟΥΣ ΚΑΙ ΛΕΓΕΙ ΑΥΤΟΙΣ ΕΓΩ ΟΥΔΕΜΙΑΝ

       Συ λέγεις ὅτι βασι-
-λευς εἰμι . ἐγω εἰς τοῦτο γεγέννημαι
και εἰς τοῦτὸ ἐλήλυθα εἰς τον κόσμον ἵνα μαρτυ-
-ρησω τῇ ἀληθείᾳ . πᾶς ὁ ὢν ἐκ τῆς ἀληθείας
ἀκούει μου.τῆς φωνῆς . λέγει αὐτῷ
ὁ Πιλᾶτος , Τί ἐστιν ἀλήθεια ; και τοῦτο
εἰπων πάλιν ἐξῆλθεν προς τους Ἰου-
-δαίους . και λέγει αὐτοῖς , Ἐγω οὐδεμίαν

5. Text of John 18:31 33 and 37 38. Transcription of the papyrus lines into upper-case letters, completing the lines as they must have looked originally; comparison with plate 3 will show how much of each line the fragment presently contains.

Transcription into lower-case letters as in a modern edition of the New Testament such as Kurt Aland's of 1967. Except for an iotacized diphthong, there is no difference between the papyrus and a modern text.

Plate 6

6. Berlin Papyrus 6845 (from W. Schubart's *Papyri Berolinenses*), showing in actual size some lines from the Iliad, Book 8 (verses 436–447, 434). A careful examination will show the striking similarity between the writing here and the writing in plates 2 and 4.

Plate 7   55

ΙΛΙΑΔΟΣ   Θ 436-447,434.

ΑΥΤΑΙ ΔΕ ΧΡΥΣ)ΕΟΙΣΙΝ ΕΠΙ ΚΛΕΙΣΜΟΙΣΙ ΚΑΘΙΖΟΝ
ΜΙΓΔ ΑΛΛΟ)ΙΣΙ ΘΕΟΙΣΙ ΦΙΛΟΝ ΤΕΤΙΗΜΕΝΑΙ ΗΤΟΡ
ΖΕΥΣ ΔΕ ΠΑ)ΤΗΡ ΙΔΗΘΕΝ ΕΥΤΡΟΧΟΝ ΑΡΜΑ ΚΑΙ ΙΠΠΟΥΣ
ΟΥΛΥΜΠΟΝ)ΔΕ ΔΙΩΚΕ ΘΕΩΝ Δ ΕΞΕΙΚΕΤΟ ΘΩΚΟΥΣ
ΤΩ ΔΕ ΚΑΙ Ι)ΠΠΟΥΣ ΜΕΝ ΛΥΣΕΝ ΚΛΥΤΟΣ ΕΝΝΟΣΙΓΑΙΟΣ
ΑΡΜΑΤΑ Δ ΑΜ) ΒΩΜΟΙΣΙ ΤΙΘΕΙ ΚΑΤΑ ΛΕΙΤΑ ΠΕΤΑΣΣΑΣ
ΑΥΤΟΣ ΔΕ ΧΡ)ΥΣΕΙΟΝ ΕΠΙ ΘΡΟΝΟΝΕΥΡΥΟΠΑ ΖΕΥΣ
ΕΖΕΤΟ ΤΩ) Δ ΥΠΟ ΠΟΣΣΙ ΜΕΓΑΣ ΠΕΛΕΜΙΖΕΤ ΟΛΥΜΠΟΣ
ΑΙ Δ ΟΙΑΙ ΔΙΟ)Σ ΑΜΦΙΣ ΑΘΗΝΑΙΗ ΤΕ ΚΑΙ ΗΡΗ
ΗΣΘΗΝ Ο)ΥΔΕ ΤΙ ΜΙΝ ΠΡΟΣΕΦΩΝΕΟΝ ΟΥΔ ΕΡΕΟΝΤΟ
ΑΥΤΑΡ Ο ΕΓ)ΝΩ ΗΣΙΝ ΕΝΙ ΦΡΕΣΙ ΦΩΝΗΣΕΝ ΤΕ
ΤΙΦΘ ΟΥΤ)Ω ΤΕΤΙΗΣΘΟΝ ΑΘΗΝΑΙΗ ΤΕ ΚΑΙ ΗΡΗ

ΚΑΙ ΤΟΥΣ) ΜΕΝ ΚΑΤΕΔΗΣΑΝ ΕΠ ΑΜΒΡΟΣΙΗΣΙ ΚΑΠΗΣΙΝ

Αὐται δε χρυσέοισιν ἐπι κλισμοῖσι καθῖζον
μιγδ'ἄλλοισι θεοῖσι, φίλον τετιημέναι ἦτορ.
Ζευς δε πατηρ ῎Ιδηθεν εὔτροχον ἅρμα και'ἵππους
Οὔλυμπόν δε δίωκε, θεῶν δ'ἐξείκετο θώκους .
Τῷ δε και ἵππους μεν λῦσε κλυτος 'Εννοσίγαιος ,
ἅρματα δ'ἄμ βωμοῖσι τίθει, κατα λεῖτα πετάσσας.
αὐτος δε χρύσειον ἐπι θρόνον εὐρύοπα Ζευς
ἔζετο . τῷ δ'ὑπο ποσσι μέγας πελεμίζετ'῎Ολυμπος.
Αἱ δ'οῖαι Διος ἀμφις 'Αθηναίη τε και ῞Ηρη
ἤσθην , οὐδέ τί μιν προσεφώνεον οὐδ' ἐρέοντο.
αὐταρ ὁ ἔγνω ᾗσιν ἐνι φρεσι , φώνησέν τε.
Τίφθ' οὕτω τετίησθον, 'Αθηναίη τε και ῞Ηρη ;

και· τους μεν κατέδησαν ἐπ' ἀμβροσίῃσι κάπῃσιν,

7. The transcription into upper-case letters gives the text as found
   in the papyrus. The lower-case text is from Pierron's edition
   (Paris: Hachette).

8. Papyrus Egerton 2, which the newspapers of 1935 were calling "The Unknown Gospel"; it dates from 150 at the latest.

Plate 9   57

ΝΟΜΕΝΟΙ·ΠΡΟΣ ΑΥΤΟΝ ΕΞ
ΤΙΚΩΣ ΕΠΕΙΡΑΖΟΝ ΑΥΤΟΝ Λ
ΔΙΔΑΣΚΑΛΕ ΙΗ   ΟΙΔΑΜΕΝ ΟΤΙ
ΕΛΗΛΥΘΑΣ Α ΓΑΡ ΠΟΙΕΙΣ ΜΑ
ΥΠΕΡ ΤΟ Σ ΠΡΟΦ(ΗΤ)ΑΣ ΠΑΝΤΑΣ
ΗΜΕΙΝ ΕΞΟΝ ΤΟΙΣ ΒΑ(ΣΙ)ΛΕΥΣ
ΝΑΙ ΤΑ Α   ΚΟΝΤΑ ΤΗ ΑΡΧΗ ΑΠ
ΤΟΙΣ Η Μ   ΟΔΕ ΙΗ ΕΙΔΩΣ
ΑΝΟΙΑΝ   ΩΝ ΕΜΒΡΕΙΜ
ΕΙΠΕΝ Α   ΤΙ ΜΕ ΚΑΛΕΙΤ
ΜΑΤΙ ΥΜ   ΔΑΣΚΑΛΟΝ Μ
ΟΝΤΕΣ Ο   ΓΩ ΚΑΛΩΣ Η
ΜΩΝ ΕΠ   ΣΕΝ ΕΙ Ν
ΤΟΣ ΤΟΙΣ   ΕΣΙΝ ΑΥ
ΜΕ Η   Α ΑΥΤ
ΧΕΙ ΑΠΕ   ΑΤΗ
  Τ

νόμενοι προς αὐτον ἐξετασ-
-τικῶς ἐπείραζον αὐτον λέγοντες
διδάσκαλε ⸗Ιησοῦ, οἴδαμεν ὅτι ἀπο Θεοῦ
ἐλήλυθας ἃ γαρ ποιεῖς μαρτυρεῖ
ὑπερ τους προφήτας πάντας λέγε οὖν
ἡμεῖν ἐξον τοῖς βασιλεῦσιν ἀποδοῦ-
-ναι τα ἀνήκοντα τῇ ἀρχῇ ἀποδῶμεν αὐ-
-τοῖς ἤ μή ὁ δε ᾿Ιησοῦς εἰδως την δι-
-άνοιαν αὐτῶν ἐμβρ(ε)ιμησάμενος
εἶπεν αὐτοῖς . Τί με καλεῖτε τῷ στό-
-ματι ὑμῶν διδάσκαλον μη ἀκού-
-οντες ὅ λέγω . καλῶς ᾿Ησ(αΐ)ας περι ὑ-
-μῶν ἐπροφήτευσεν εἰπων .ὁ λαός οὑ-
-τος τοῖς χείλεσιν αὐτῶν τιμῶσιν
με,ἡ δε καρδία αὐτῶν πόρρω ἀπε-
-χει ἀπ᾿ἐμοῦ μάτην με σέβονται
ἐντάλματα.

9. Transcription of the recto side into upper-case letters. The missing letters are filled in in the lower-case transcription.

10. Berlin Papyrus 6854 (photograph 34 in Schubart's *Palaeo-graphie*). The text is a complaint addressed to Trajan between 98 and 117. Compare the writing here with that in the Manchester Papyrus.

Plate 11   59

KY	κύ-
ΡΙΟΝ ΤΗ Δ ΤΟΥ ΕΝΕΣ	-ριον τῇ δ τοῦ ἐνεσ-
ΤΩΤΟΣ ΜΗΝΟΣ ΦΑΡΜΟΥΘΙ	-τῶτος μηνος Φαρμοῦθι
ΑΠΛΩΣ ΜΗΔΕΝ ΕΧΟΥΣΑ	ἁπλῶς μηδεν ἔχουσα
ΠΡΑΓΜΑ ΠΡΟΣ ΕΜΕ ΤΑΟΡΣΕ	πρᾶγμα προς ἐμε Ταορσε-
ΝΟΥΦΙΣ ΓΥΝΗ ΑΜΜΩΝΙΟΥ	-νοῦφις γυνη ᾿Αμμωνίου
ΤΟΥ ΚΑΙ ΦΙΜΩΝΟΣ ΠΡΕΣΒΥ	τοῦ και Φίμωνος πρεσβυ-
ΤΕΡΟΥ ΚΩΜΗΣ ΒΑΚΧΙΑΔΟ(Σ)	-τέρου κώμης Βακχιάδο(ς)
ΕΠΕΛΘΟΥΣΑ ΕΝ ΤΗΝ ΟΙ	ἐπελθοῦσα ἐν την οἰ-
ΚΙΑ ΜΟΥ ΑΛΟΓΟΝ ΜΟΙ ΑΗ	-κίᾳ μου ἄλογόν μοι ἀη-
ΔΙΑΝ ΣΥΝΕΣΤΗΣΑΤΟ ΚΑΙ	-δίαν συνεστήσατο και
ΠΕΡΙΕΣΧΙΣΕ ΜΟΙ ΤΟΝ ΚΙ	περιέσχισέ μοι τον κι-
ΤΩΝΑ ΚΑΙ ΤΟ ΠΑΛΛΙΟΝ	-τῶνα και το πάλλιον
ΟΥ ΜΟΝΟΝ ΑΛΛΑ ΚΑΙ ΑΠΕ	οὐ μόνον ἀλλα και ἀπε-
ΝΕΓΚΑΤΟ ΜΟΥ ΕΝ ΤΗ ΑΗ	-νέγκατό μου ἐν τῇ ἀη-
ΔΙΑ ΑΣ ΕΙΧΟΝ ΚΙΜΕΝΑΣ	-δίᾳ ἅς εἴχον κιμένας
ΑΠΟ ΤΙΜΗΣ ΩΝ ΠΕΠΡΑΚΟΝ	ἀπο τιμῆς ὧν πέπρακον
ΛΑΧΑΝΩΝ Σ ΙΣ ΚΑΙ ΤΗ	λαχάνων Σ ις και τῇ
Ε ΤΟΥ ΑΥΤΟΥ ΜΗΝΟΣ	ε τοῦ αὐτοῦ μηνος
ΕΠΕΛΘΩΝ Ο ΤΑΥΤΗΣ	ἐπελθων ὁ ταύτης
ΑΝΗΡ ΑΜΜΩΝΙΟΣ Ο ΚΑΙ ΦΙ	ἀνηρ ᾿Αμμώνιος ὁ και Φί-
ΜΩΝ ΕΙΣ ΤΗΝ ΟΙΚΙΑΝ ΜΟΥ	-μων εἰς την οἰκίαν μου

11. Transcription into modern upper-case letters to imitate the capital letters of the papyrus; transcription into lower-case letters to facilitate the reading of it.

12. Berlin Greek Papyrus 173. Letter of an official under Hadrian in
135. The papyrus has been damaged, but the ink is very clear
under a magnifying glass, and the chancery hand is quite regular.

Plate 13   61

```
ΚΛΑΥΔΙ)ΟΣ ΦΙΛΟΞΕΝΟΣ ΝΕΩΚΟΡΟΣ ΤΟΥ ΜΕΓΑΛΟΥ
ΣΑΡΑ)ΠΙΔΟΣ ΓΕΝΟΜΕΝΟΣ ΕΠΑΡΧΟΣ ΣΠΕΙ
ΡΗΣ ) ΠΡΩΤΗΣ ΔΑΜΑΣΚΗΝΩΝ ΤΩΝ ΕΝ
ΤΩΙ )ΜΟΥΣΕΙΩΙ ΣΕΙΤΟΥΜΕΝΩΝ ΑΤΕΛΩΝ
ΙΕΡ)ΕΥΣ ΚΑΙ ΑΡΧΙΔΙΚΑΣΤΗΣ  ΑΡΧΙΑΙ
ΣΤΡ)ΑΤΗΓΩΙ ΑΡΣΙΝΟΕΙΤΟΥ ΤΩΙ
ΤΙΜΙ)ΩΤΑΤΩΙ   ΧΑΙΡΕΙΝ  .
ΒΙΒΛΙ)ΔΙΟΝ ΙΟΥΛΙΟΥ ΑΓΡΙΠΠΙΝΟΥ
ΣΗΜΕ)ΙΩΣΑΜΕΝΟΣ ΕΠΕΜΨΑ ΣΟΙ ΕΑΝ  ...


Κλαύδι)ος Φιλόξενος νεωκόρος τοῦ μεγάλου
Σαρά)πιδος γενόμενος ἔπαρχος σπει-
-ρης ) πρώτης  Δαμα(σ)κηνῶν τῶν ἐν
τῷ ) Μουσείῳ σειτουμένων ἀτελῶν
ἱερ)ευς και ἀρχιδικαστης 'Αρχίαι
στρ)ατηγῷ 'Αρσινοείτου  τῷ
τιμι)ωτάτῳ ,  χαίρειν.
βιβλί)διον 'Ιουλίου 'Αγριππιανοῦ
σημε)ιωσάμενος ἔπεμψα σοι ἐαν ....
```

13. A transcription of the previous into upper- and lower-case letters, first letters of each line being completed before the parenthesis.

14. Facade of the John Rylands Library, Deansgate, Manchester; an admirable building in late Gothic style, opened by Mrs. Rylands in 1899 in honor of her husband who had made his fortune in this industrial city. The library has almost a million volumes and ten thousand manuscripts, making it an oasis for historical research amid its industrial surroundings.

Plate 15   63

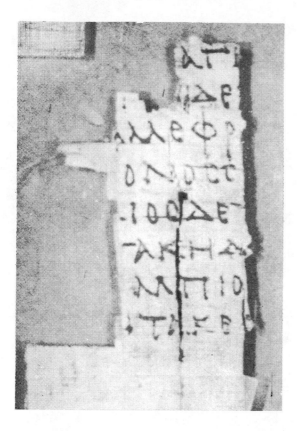

āγ

δε

αμε φρ

ον οσσ

Διος δε

γα κηδ

μπιο

ν τα κε θ

ΙΛΙΑΔΟΣ 24 (169–175)

Στῆ δε παρα Πρΐαμον Διος ἄγγελος , ἡδε προσηΰδα,

τυτθον φθεγξαμένη . τον δε τρόμος ἔλλαβε γυῖα.

θάρσει ,Δαρδανΐδη Πρΐαμε, φρεσι, μηδέ τι τάρβει.

Οὐ μεν γἀρ τοι ἐγω κακον ὀσσομένη τόδ'ἱκἀνω ,

ἀλλ'ἀγαθα φρονέουσα . Διος δέ τοι ἄγγελός εἰμι,

ὅς σευ ἄνευθεν ἐων μέγα κήδεται ἡδ'ἐλεαΐρει.

Λΰσασθαΐ σ'ἐκελευσεν 'Ολυμπιος "Εκτορα δῖον,

δῶρα δ' 'Αχιλλῆι φερέμεν ,τἀ κε θυμον ἱήνῃ,

15. Fragment 544 of Manchester with its thirty-five letters of Iliad text, certainly dating from the end of the first century; with transcriptions.

Plate 16

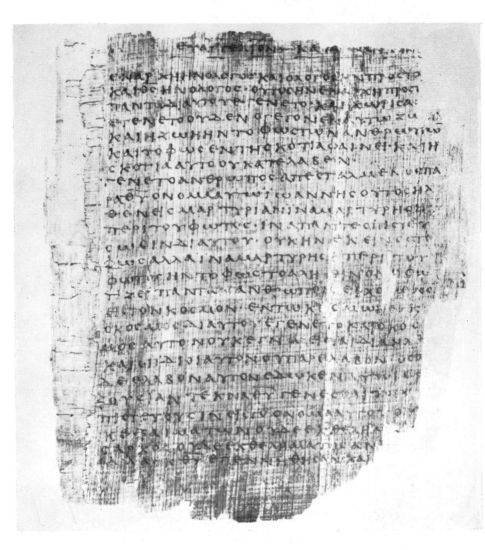

16. Papyrus Bodmer II, at Cologny-Geneva; first page of the Fourth
Gospel; 200 A.D.

Plate 17 65

ΕΥΑΓΓΕΛΙΟΝ ΚΑΤΑ ΙΩΑΝΝΗΝ . Ι .(1–13)·

'Εν ἀρχῇ ἦν ὁ λόγος ,και ὁ λόγος ἦν προς το(ν Θεόν)

και Θεος ἦν ὁ λόγος . οὗτος ἦν ἐν ἀρχῇ προς τ(ον Θεόν)

πάντα δι'αὐτοῦ ἐγένετο, και χωρις α(ὐτοῦ)

ἐγένετο οὐδεν . ὅ γέγονεν ἐν αὐτῷ ζωη (ἦν)

και ἡ ζωη ἦν το φῶς τῶν ἀνθρώπων

και το φῶς ἐν τῇ σκοτίᾳ φαίνει ,και ἡ

σκοτία αὐτο οὐ κατέλαβεν .

'Εγένετο ἄνθρωπος ἀπεσταλμένος πα-

-ρα Θεοῦ ,ὄνομα αὐτῷ 'Ιωάννης .οὗτος ἦλ-

-θεν εἰς μαρτυρίαν, ἵνα μαρτυρήσῃ

περι τοῦ φωτός, ἵνα πάντες πιστεύ-

-σωσιν δι'αὐτοῦ. οὐκ ἦν ἐκεῖνος το

φῶς ,ἀλλα ἵνα μαρτυρήσῃ περι τοῦ

φωτός . ῏Ην το φῶς το ἀληθινόν, ὅ φω-

-τίζει πάντα ἄνθρωπον ἐρχόμενον

εἰς τον κόσμον .ἐν τῷ κόσμῳ ἦν ; και·

ὁ κόσμος δι'αὐτοῦ ἐγένετο και ὁ κόσ-

-μος αὐτον οὐκ ἔγνω. εἰς τα ἴδια ἦλθεν,

και οἱ ἴδιοι αὐτον οὐ παρέλαβον . ὅσοι

δε ἔλαβον αὐτον , ἔδωκεν αὐτοῖς ἐ-

-ξουσίαν τέκνα Θεοῦ γενέσθαι ,τοῖς

πιστεύουσιν εἰς το ὄνομα αὐτοῦ ,οἱ οὐ-

-κ ἐξ αἱμάτων οὐδε ἐκ θελήμα(τος)

σαρκος οὐδε ἐκ θελήματος ἀν(δρος)

ἀλλα ἐκ Θ(εο)ῦ ἐγεννήθησαν .

17. Lower-case transcription of the first thirteen verses of John in the Papyrus Bodmer II.

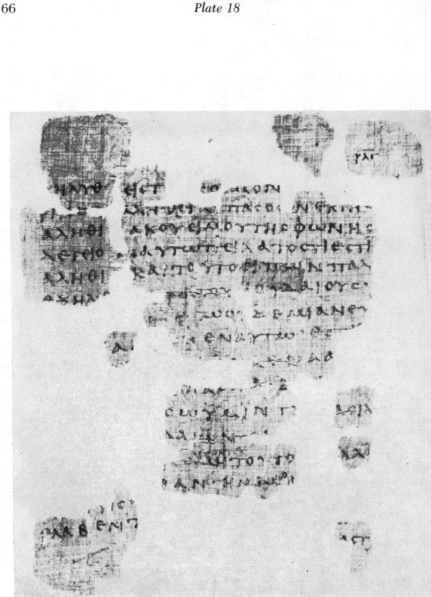

18. Fragments of Papyrus Bodmer II covering same verses as found
in plate 5 (bottom half).

Plate 19   67

KATA ΙΩΑΝΝΗΝ   18   (37-40)

```
ΗΛΥΘ   ΕΙΣ Τ              ΙΝΑ ΜΑΡΤΥ
ΡΗΣΩ    ΑΛΗΘΕΙΑ ΠΑΣ Ο ΩΝ ΕΚ ΤΗ
ΑΛΗΘΕΙ   ΑΚΟΥΕΙ ΜΟΥ ΤΗΣ ΦΩΝΗΣ
ΛΕΓΕΙ Ο   ΑΥΤΩ Ο ΠΕΙΛΑΤΟΣ ΤΙ ΕΣΤΙΝ
ΑΛΗΘ      ΚΑΙ ΤΟΥΤΟ ΕΙΠΩΝ ΠΑΛΙΝ
ΕΞΗΛ      ΟΣ ΤΟΥ   ΙΟΥΔΑΙΟΥΣ
                    ΕΓΩ ΟΥΔΕΜΙΑΝ ΕΥ
         ΑΙ   ΑΝ ΕΝ ΑΥΤΩ   ΕΣΤΙΝ
                  ΝΑ ΕΝΑ
                  ΠΑΣΧΑ
               ΣΩ ΥΜΙΝ ΤΟ   ΒΑΣΙ
               ΔΑΙΩΝ  ΕΚ
                  λεγοντες
               ΜΗ ΤΟΥΤ   ΛΛ
               ΒΑΝ ΗΝ ΔΕ
         ΤΗΣ
         ΕΛΑΒΕΝ
```

```
              (εἰς τοῦτο ἐ-)
-λήλυθα εἰς τον κόσμον ἵνα μαρτυ-
-ρήσω τῇ ἀληθείᾳ . πᾶς ὁ ὤν ἐκ τῆς.
ἀληθείας ἀκούει μου τῆς φωνῆς.
λέγει οὖν αὐτῷ ὁ Πειλᾶτος :Τί ἐστιν
ἀλήθεια ; καὶ τοῦτο εἰπων πάλιν
ἐξῆλθεν προς τους ᾽Ιουδαίους
καὶ λέγει αὐτοῖς :᾽Εγω οὐδεμίαν εὑ-
-ρίσκω αἰτίαν ἐν αὐτῷ . ἔστιν
δε συνήθεια ὑμῖν ἵνα ἕνα ἀπο-
-λύσω ὑμῖν ἐν τῷ πάσχα . βούλεσ-
-θε οὖν ἀπολύσω ὑμῖν τον βασιλέα
τῶν ᾽Ιουδαίων ; ἐκραύγασαν οὖν
              (λέγοντεσ)
πάλιν πάντες . μη τοῦτον ἀλλα
τον βαραββᾶν . ἦν δε βαραββᾶς
λῃστής . 19 . Τότε οὖν ὁ Πειλᾶτος
ἔλαβεν τον ᾽Ιησοῦν καὶ ἐμάστιγω-
-σεν .
```

19. Transcription in capital letters of the letters in these fragments.
The complete text is given in lower-case letters (note insertion of
Greek particle "saying" between the twelfth and thirteenth
lines).

20. First page of the codex of the Fourth Gospel in Papyrus 75 (i.e., Bodmer XV), published in 1961. Date: 175–225.

Plate 21 . 69

Πάπυρος 7 5 .

ΕΥΑΓΓΕΛΙΟΝ ΚΑΤΑ ΙΩΑΝΗΝ .
'Εν ἀρχῇ ἦν ὁ λόγος και ὁ λόγος ἦν προς τον
Θ(εὸ)ν και Θ(εο)ς ἦν ὁ λόγος . οὗτος ἦν ἐν ἀρχῇ προς
τον Θ(εὸ)ν . πάντα δι'αὐτοῦ ἐγένετο και χωρις
αὐτοῦ ἐγένετο οὐδε ἕν ὅ γέγονεν ἐν αὐτῷ
ζωη ἦν και ἡ ζωη ἦν το φῶς τῶν ἀν(θρώπ)ων
και το φῶς ἐν τῇ σκοτείᾳ φαίνει και ἡ σκο—
—τεία αὐτο οὐ κατέλαβεν . ἐγένετο ἄνθρω—
—πος ἀπεσταλμένος παρα Θ(εο)ῦ ,ὄνομα αὐτῷ
'Ιωάνης , οὗτος ἦλθεν εἰς μαρτυρίον ἵνα
μαρτυρήσῃ περι τοῦ φωτός ἵνα πάν—
—τες πιστεύσωσιν δι'αὐτοῦ . οὐκ ἦν ἐκεῖ—
—νος το φῶς ἀλλ'ἵνα μαρτυρήσῃ περι τοῦ
φωτός ,ἦν το φῶς το ἀληθινόν ὅ φωτί—
—ζει πάντα ἄν(θρωπ)ον ἐρχόμενον εἰς τον κό—
—σμον .ἐν τῷ κόσμῳ ἦν και ὁ κόσμος δι'
αὐτοῦ ἐγένετο και ὁ κόσμος αὐτον οὐκ
ἔγνω , εἰς τα ἴδια ἦλθεν και οἱ ἴδιοι αὐ—
—τον οὐ παρέλαβον . ὅσοι δε ἔλαβον αὐτόν
ἔδωκεν αὐτοῖς ἐξουσίαν τέκνα Θ(εο)ῦ γε—
—νέσθαι τοῖς πιστεύουσιν εἰς το ὄνομα αὐ—
—τοῦ ,οἴ οὐκ ἐξ αἱμάτων οὐδε ἐκ θελήμα—
—τος σαρκος οὐδε ἐκ θελήματος ἀνδρος
ἀλλ'ἐκ Θ(εο)ῦ ἐγενήθησαν . και ὁ λόγος σαρξ ἐ—
—γένετο και ἐσκήνωσεν ἐν ἡμῖν και ἐθε—
—ασάμεθα την δόξαν αὐτοῦ , δόξαν ὡς μο—
—νογενοῦς παρα πατρός πλήρης χάριτος και
ἀληθείας .'Ιωανης μαρτυρεῖ περι αὐτοῦ
και κέκραγε λέγων , οὗτος ἦν ὅν εἶπον ὁ
ὀπίσω μου ἐρχόμενος ἔμπροσθέν μου
γέγονεν ὅτι πρῶτός μου ἦν ὅτι ἐκ τοῦ ....

21. Lower-case transcription of first fifteen verses. The abbreviations of the sacred names are filled out in parentheses.

22. The Chester Beatty fragment of the Fourth Gospel (Dublin).
Date: 250.

Plate 23   71

ΙΩΑΝΝΗΣ Χ, (31-42) - ΧΙ, (1-10) .

'Εγω καὶ ὁ Πατηρ ἕν ἐσμε)ν. 'Εβάστασαν (λ(θους
οἱ 'Ιουδ)αῖοι ἴνα λιθάσωσιν (αὐτόν .ἀπ)εκρ(θη αὐτοῖς (ὁ 'Ιησοῦςπολλα
ἔργα κα)λα ἔδειξα ὑμῖν (ἐκ τοῦ ΠΡΣ .δια)ποῖον αὐτῶν ἔργον ἐμε
λιθά)ζετε ; ἀπεκρ(θησαν (αὐτῷ οἱ 'Ιο)οδαῖοι ,Περι καλοῦ ἔργου οὐ λι-
-θάζο)μέν σε ἀλλα περι βλασφημίας , καὶ ὅτι συ ἄνθρωπος ὢν
ποιε)ῖς σεαυτον θεον . Απεκρίθη αὐτοῖς ὁ· 'ΙΗ ,οὐκ ἔστιν γεγραμμένον
ἐν τῇ γραφῇ .ἐν τῷ νόμῳ.ὅτι 'Εγω εἶπα θεοί ἐστε ;εἰ ἐκείνους εἶ-
-πεν θ)εους καὶ οὐ δύναται λυθῆναι ὅν ὁ πατηρ ἡγίασεν καὶ ἀπέστει-
-λεν εἰς)τον κόσμον ὑμεῖς λέγετε ὅτι εἶπον ὁ Υ(ἱος)
τοῦ ΘΥ)εἰμι ; εἰ οὐ ποιῶ τα ἔργα τοῦ ΠΡΣ μου, μη πιστεύετέ μοι εἰδε
ποιῶ,)κἂν ἐμοι μη πιστεύητε, τοῖς ἔργοις πιστεύετε, ἴνα γνῶτε
καὶ γ)ινώσκητε ὅτι ἐν ἐμοι ὁ ΠΡ κἀγω ἐν αὐτῳ. 'Εζήτουν δε αὐτον
πιάσαι κ)αι ἐξῆλθεν ἐκ τῆς χειρος αὐτῶν. καὶ ἀπῆλθεν πάλιν πέ-
-ραν το)ῦ 'Ιορδάνου εἰς τον τόπον ὅπου ἦν 'Ιωάννης το πρότερον βα-
-πτίζω)ν καὶ ἔμεινεν ἐκεῖ .καὶ πολλοι ἦλθον προς αὐτον καὶ ἔλε-
-γον ὅτι) 'Ιωάννης μεν σημεῖον ἐποίησεν οὐδε ἕν ,πάντα δε ὅσα
'Ιωάνν)ης εἶπεν περι τούτου ἀληθῆ ἦν . καὶ πολλοι ἐπίστευσαν εἰς
αὐτον . ᾞΗν)δε τις ἀσθενῶν , Λάζαρος ἀπο Βηθανίαμ ἐκ τῆς κώμης
Μαρίας)καὶ Μάρθας τῆς ἀδελφῆς αὐτῆς . ἦν δε αὐτή ἡ Μαρ(ία ἡ
ἀλείψασα το)ν ΚΝ μύρῳ καὶ ἐκμ(άξασ)α τους πόδας αὐτοῦ ταῖς θρι-
-ξιν αὐτῆς ἧς) ὁ ἀδελφος Λάζαρ ἠ(σθέ)νει .ἀπέστειλαν (οὖ)ν αἱ ἀδελ-
-φαι προς αὐτον λέγο)υσαι .ΚΕ ἴδε ὅν φιλεῖς ἀσθενεῖ.ἀκούσας δ(ε ὁ ΙΗ
εἶπεν ,αὕτη ἡ ἀ)σθένεια οὐκ ἔστιν προς θάνατον. ἀλλ(ὑπερ
τῆς δόξης το)ῦ ΘΥ ἴνα δοξασθῇ ὁ ΥΣ αὐτοῦ δι'αὐτῆς .ἠγάπ(α δε
ὁ ΙΗ την Μάρθαν)καὶ την ἀδελφην αὐτῆς καὶ τον Λάζαρον (ὡς οὖν
ἤκουσεν ὅτι)ἀσθενεῖ . τότε μεν ἔμεινεν ἐπι τῷ τόπῳ
β ἡμέρας .ἔιτα)μετα τοῦτο λέγε(ι ἄγ)ωμεν εἰς την 'Ιουδα(ίαν πάλιν λέγουσιν α)ὐτῷ οἱ μαθητα(ὶ ῥαββεὶ νῦν ἐζήτουν σε λ(ιθάσαι
οἱ 'Ιουδαῖοι καὶ π)άλιν ὑπάγεις (ἐκεῖ.ἀπεκρίθη ὁ ΙΗ οὐχι δώ(δεκα
ὦραι εἰσιν τῆς) ἡμέρας ;ἐάν (τις ἐν τῇ) ἡμέρᾳ περιπατῇ (οὐ προσ-
κόπτει ὅτι το φ)ῶς τοῦ κ(όσμου τούτο βλέπει .ἐαν δε τις) περιπ(ατῇ

23. Lower-case transcription of John 10:31–11:10. Words missing at the beginning of lines are completed in front of the parenthesis; missing words or letters within lines are completed within parentheses.

24. Codex Vaticanus 1209, from fourth century (ca. 325); chapter 18, telling of Jesus before Pilate.

Plate 25 73

2

TO ΠΡΑΙΤΩΡΙΟΝ ΙΝΑ ΜΗ
ΜΙΑΝΘΩΣΙΝ ΑΛΛΑ ΦΑΓΩ
ΣΙΝ ΤΟ ΠΑΣΧΑ ΕΞΗΛΘΕΝ
ΟΥΝ Ο ΠΕΙΛΑΤΟΣ ΕΞΩ
ΠΡΟΣ ΑΥΤΟΥΣ ΚΑΙ ΦΗΣΙΝ
ΤΙΝΑ ΚΑΤΗΓΟΡΙΑΝ ΦΕΡΕ
ΤΕ ΤΟΥ ΑΝΘΡΩΠΟΥ ΤΟΥ
ΤΟΥ ΑΠΕΚΡΙΘΗΣΑΝ ΚΑΙ
ΕΙΠΑΝ ΑΥΤΩ ΕΙ ΜΗ ΗΝ ΟΥ
ΤΟΣ ΚΑΚΟΝ ΠΟΙΩΝ ΟΥΚ ΑΝ
ΣΟΙ ΠΑΡΕΔΩΚΑΜΕΝ ΑΥΤΟΝ
ΕΙΠΕΝ ΟΥΝ ΑΥΤΟΙΣ ΠΕΙΛΑ
ΤΟΣ ΛΑΒΕΤΕ ΑΥΤΟΝ ΥΜΕΙΣ
ΚΑΙ ΚΑΤΑ ΤΟΝ ΝΟΜΟΝ Υ
ΜΩΝ ΚΡΕΙΝΑΤΕ ΑΥΤΟΝ
ΕΙΠΟΝ ΑΥΤΩ ΟΙ ΙΟΥΔΑΙΟΙ
ΗΜΙΝ ΟΥΚ ΕΞΕΣΤΙΝ ΑΠΟ
ΚΤΕΙΝΑΙ ΟΥΔΕΝΑ ΙΝΑ Ο
ΛΟΓΟΣ ΤΟΥ ΙΥ ΠΛΗΡΩΘΗ
ΟΝ ΕΙΠΕΝ ΣΗΜΑΙΝΩΝ ΠΟΙ
Ω ΘΑΝΑΤΩ ΗΜΕΛΛΕΝ Α
ΠΟΘΝΗΣΚΕΙΝ ΕΙΣΗΛ
ΘΕΝ ΟΥΝ ΠΑΛΙΝ ΕΙΣ ΤΟ ΠΡΑΙ
ΤΩΡΙΟΝ Ο ΠΕΙΛΑΤΟΣ ΚΑΙ
ΕΦΩΝΗΣΕΝ ΤΟΝ ΙΝ ΚΑΙ
ΕΙΠΕΝ ΑΥΤΩ ΣΥ ΕΙ Ο ΒΑΣΙ
ΛΕΥΣ ΤΩΝ ΙΟΥΔΑΙΩΝ
ΑΠΕΚΡΙΘΗ ΙΣ ΑΠΟ ΣΕΑΥ
ΤΟΥ ΣΥ ΤΟΥΤΟ ΛΕΓΕΙΣ Η
ΑΛΛΟΙ ΕΙΠΟΝ ΣΟΙ ΠΕΡΙ ΕΜΟΥ
ΑΠΕΚΡΙΘΗ Ο ΠΕΙΛΑΤΟΣ
ΜΗ ΤΙ ΕΓΩ ΙΟΥΔΑΙΟΣ ΕΙΜΙ
ΤΟ ΕΘΝΟΣ ΤΟ ΣΟΝ ΚΑΙ ΟΙ
ΑΡΧΙΕΡΕΙΣ ΠΑΡΕΔΩΚΑΝ
ΣΕ ΕΜΟΙ ΤΙ ΕΠΟΙΗΣΑΣ
ΑΠΕΚΡΙΘΗ ΙΣ Η ΒΑΣΙΛΕΙΑ
Η ΕΜΗ ΟΥΚ ΕΣΤΙΝ ΕΚ ΤΟΥ
ΚΟΣΜΟΥ ΤΟΥΤΟΥ ΕΙ ΕΚ ΤΟΥ
ΚΟΣΜΟΥ ΤΟΥΤΟΥ ΗΝ Η ΒΑ
ΣΙΛΕΙΑ Η ΕΜΗ ΟΙ ΥΠΗΡΕΤΑΙ
ΟΙ ΕΜΟΙ ΗΓΩΝΙΖΟΝΤΟ ΑΝ Ι
ΝΑ ΜΗ ΠΑΡΑΔΟΘΩ ΤΟΙΣ

3

'Ιουδαίοις νῦν δε ἡ βασι-
-λεία ἡ ἐμη οὐκ ἔστιν ἐν-
-τεῦθεν .εἶπεν οὖν αὐ-
-τῷ ὁ Πειλᾶτος οὐκοῦν
βασιλευς εἶ σύ ; ἀπεκρί-
-θη ὁ ΙΣ ,συ λέγεις ὅτι βα-
-σιλεύς εἰμι ἐγω εἰς τοῦ-
-το γεγέννημαι και
εἰς τοῦτο ἐλήλυθα
εἰς τον κόσμον ἵνα μαρ-
-τυρήσω τῇ ἀληθείᾳ .πᾶς
ὁ ὢν ἐκ τῆς ἀληθείας ἀ-
-κούει μου τῆς φωνῆς
λέγει αὐτῷ ὁ Πειλᾶτος
Τί ἐστιν ἀλήθεια ; και τοῦ-
-το εἰπων ,πάλιν ἐξῆλθεν
προς τους 'Ιουδαίους και
λέγει αὐτοῖς .'Εγω οὐδε-
-μίαν εὑρίσκω ἐν αὐτῷ
αἰτίαν .ἔστιν δε συνή-
-θεια ὑμῖν ἵνα ἕνα ἀπο-
-λύσω ὑμῖν τῷ πασχα .
βούλεσθε οὖν ἀπολύσω
ὑμῖν τον βασιλέα τῶν
'Ιουδαίων ;ἐκραύγασαν
οὖν πάλιν λέγοντες ,
μη τοῦτον ἀλλα τον βα-
-ραββᾶν . ἦν δε ὁ βαραββᾶς
λῃστής. 19 .Τότε οὖν ἔ-
-λαβεν ὁ Πειλᾶτος τον
'ΙΝ και ἐμαστείγωσεν .
και οἱ στρατιῶται πλέ-
-ξαντες στέφανον
ἐξ ἀκανθῶν ἐπέθηκαν
αὐτοῦ τῇ κεφαλῇ και
ἱμάτιον πορφυροῦν
περιέβαλον αὐτόν , και
ἤρχοντο προς αὐτον
και ἔλεγον . Χαῖρε, ὁ βασι-
-λευς τῶν 'Ιουδαίων και
ἐδίδοσαν αὐτῷ ῥαπί-
-σματα . και ἐξῆλθεν πάλιν

25. Upper-case transcriptions of column 2 (John 18:28-36); lower-case transcription of column 3 (John 18:37-40; 19:1-4).

26. Codex Sinaiticus, discovered 1845–1859; John 18:25-40; 19:1-13. The signs and divisions in the margins are later additions.

27. Complete transcription of columns 1 and 2.

Plate 27 75

(25-33)

(33-38)

-θητῶν αὐτοῦ εἶ ;
ἠρνήσατο ἐκεῖνος
καὶ εἶπεν ,Οὐκ εἰμί.
λέγει εἷς ἐκ τῶν
δούλων τοῦ ἀρχι-
-ερέως , συνγενης
ὤν οὐ ἀπέκοψεν
Πέτρος τὸ ὠτίον ,
οὐκ ἐγώ σε ἴδον ἐν
τῷ κήπῳ μετ'αὐτοῦ ;
πάλιν οὖν ἠρνήσα--
-το ὁ Πέτρος καὶ εὐ-
-θέως ἀλέκτωρ ἐ-
-φώνησεν . Ἄγουσιν
οὖν τον Ι Ν ἀπο τοῦ
Καϊάφα εἰς το πραι-
-τώριον . ἦν δε πρω-
-ΐ . καὶ αὐτοι οὐκ εἰσῆλ-
-θον εἰς το πραιτώ-
-ριον ἵνα μη μιαν-
-θῶσιν ἀλλα φάγωσιν
το πάσχα . ἐξῆλθεν
οὖν προς αὐτους
ὁ Πιλᾶτος ἔξω καὶ
φησίν ,Τίνα κατη-
-γορίαν φέρετε κατα τοῦ
ἀνθρώπου τούτου ;
ἀπεκρίθησαν καὶ
εἶπαν αὐτῷ , εἰ μη
ἦν οὗτος κακον
ποιήσας οὐκ ἄν
σοι παρεδώκει-
-μεν αὐτόν . εἶπεν
οὖν αὐτοῖς ὁ Πιλᾶ-
-τος , Λάβετε αὐτον
ὑμῖς καὶ κατα τον
νόμον ὑμῶν κρί═
-νατε . εἶπον οὖν
αὐτῷ οἱ Ἰουδαῖοι ,
Ἡμῖν οὐκ ἔξεστιν
ἀποκτῖναι οὐδέ-
-να (οὐδένα) ἵνα
ὁ λόγος τοῦ Ι Υ πλη-
-ρωθῇ σημαίνων
ποίῳ θανάτῳ ἤ-
-μελλεν ἀποθνί-
-σκιν . Εἰσῆλθεν
οὖν εἰς το πραιτώ-

-ριον πάλιν ὁ Πιλᾶ-
-τος καὶ ἐφώνη-
-σεν τον Ι Ν καὶ εἶ-
-πεν αὐτῷ , Συ εἶ ὁ
βασιλευς τῶν Ἰου-
-δαίων ; ἀπεκρίθη
αὐτῷ ὁ ΙΣ , ἀπο σε-
-αυτοῦ τοῦτο εἶ-
-πας ἤ ἄλλοι σοι εἶ-
-πον περι ἐμοῦ ;
ἀπεκρίθη ὁ Πιλᾶ-
-τος , Μή ἐγω Ἰου-
-δαῖός εἰμι ; το ἔθνος
το σον καὶ ὁ ἀρχιε-
-ερευς παρέδωκάν
σε ἐμοί . Τί ἐποίη-
-σας ; ἀπεκρίθη ΙΣ , Ἡ
ἐμη βασιλεία
οὐκ ἔστιν ἐκ τοῦ
κόσμου τούτου .
εἰ ἐκ τοῦ κόσμου
τούτου ἦν ἡ ἐμη
βασιλία καὶ οἱ ὑπη-
-ρέται οἱ ἐμοι ἠγω-
-νίζοντο ἄν ἵνα
μη παραδοθῶ
τοῖς Ἰουδαίοις . νῦν
δε ἡ ἐμη βασιλεί-
-α οὐκ ἔστιν ἐντεῦ-
-θεν . εἶπον οὖν
αὐτῷ ὁ Πιλᾶτος,
Οὐκοῦν βασιλευς εἶ
σύ ; ἀπεκρίθη ὁ ΙΣ ,
Συ λέγεις ὅτι βασι-
-λευς εἰμι . ἐγω εἰς
τοῦτο γεγέννη-
-μαι καὶ εἰς τοῦτο
ἐλήλυθα εἰς τον
κόσμον ἵνα μαρ-
-τυρήση(ω)•περι τῆς
ἀληθίας . πᾶς ὁ ὤν
τῆς ἀληθίας ἀκού-
-ει μου τῆς φω-
-νῆς . λέγει αὐτῷ
ὁ Πιλᾶτος , Τί ἐστι
ἀλήθεια ;
καὶ τοῦτο εἰπων
πάλιν ἐξῆλθεν

ΠΡΟϹΤΟΥϹΙΟΥΛΑΝ
ΟΥϹΚΑΙΛΕΓΕΙΑΥ
ΤΟΙϹΕΓΩΟΥΛΕΜΙ
ΑΝΑΙΤΙΑΝΕΥΡΙⲕ
ΕΝΑΥΤΩΕϹΤΙΝ
ϹΥΝΗΘΙΑΥΜΙΝΙ
ΝΑΕΝΝΑΠΟΛΥ
ΥΜΙΝΕΝΤΩΠΑϹΧ
ΒΟΥΛΕϹΘΕΟΥΝΙΝΑ
ΑΠΟΛΥϹΩΥΜΙΝΤ
ΒΑϹΙΛΕΑΤΩΝΙΟΥ
ΛΑΙΩΝΕΚΡΑΥΓΑϹΑ
ΟΥΝΠΑΛΙΝΛΕΓΟΝ
ΤΕϹΜΗΤΟΥΤΟΝ·
ΑΛΛΑΤΟΝΒΑΡΑΒΒΑ
ΗΝΔΕΟΒΑΡΑΒΒΑϹΛΗ
ϹΤΗϹΤΟΤΕΟΥΝΛΑ
ΒΩΝΟΠΙΛΑΤΟϹΤ
ΙΝΕΜΑϹΤΙΓΩϹΕΝ
ΚΑΙΟΙϹΤΡΑΤΙΩΤΑΝ

28. Codex Sinaiticus: four versus from the top of column 3 in plate 26, magnified to show detail of the writing.

Plate 29   77

1 8 (38-40) - 1 9 , 1 .

ΠΡΟΣ ΤΟΥΣ ΙΟΥΔΑΙ	προς τους 'Ιουδαι-
ΟΥΣ ΚΑΙ ΛΕΓΕΙ ΑΥ	-ους και λέγει αὐ-
ΤΟΙΣ ΕΓΩ ΟΥΔΕΜΙ	-τοῖς , 'Εγω οὐδεμι-
ΑΝ ΑΙΤΙΑΝ ΕΥΡΙΣΚΩ	-αν αἰτίαν εὐρίσκω
ΕΝ ΑΥΤΩ ΕΣΤΙΝ ΔΕ	ἐν αὐτῷ . ἔστιν δε
ΣΥΝΗΘΙΑ ΥΜΙΝ Ι	συνήθια ὑμῖν ἵ-
ΝΑ ΕΝΑ ΑΠΟΛΥΣΩ	-να ἔνα ἀπολύσω
ΥΜΙΝ ΕΝ ΤΩ ΠΑΣΧΑ	ὑμῖν ἐν τῷ πάσχα .
ΒΟΥΛΕΣΘΕ ΟΥΝ ΙΝΑ	βούλεσθε οὖν ἵνα
ΑΠΟΛΥΣΩ ΥΜΙΝ ΤΟΝ	ἀπολύσω ὑμῖν τον
ΒΑΣΙΛΕΑ ΤΩΝ ΙΟΥ	βασιλέα τῶν 'Ιου-
ΔΑΙΩΝ ΕΚΡΑΥΓΑΣΑΝ	-δαίων ; ἐκραύγασαν
ΟΥΝ ΠΑΛΙΝ ΛΕΓΟΝ	οὖν πάλιν λέγον-
ΤΕΣ ΜΗ ΤΟΥΤΟΝ	-τες , μη τοῦτον
ΑΛΛΑ ΤΟΝ ΒΑΡΑΒΒΑΝ	ἀλλα τον βαραββᾶν .
ΗΝ ΔΕ Ο ΒΑΡΑΒΒΑΣ ΛΗ	ἦν δε ὁ βαραββᾶς λη-
ΣΤΗΣ . ΤΟΤΕ ΟΥΝ ΛΑ	-στής . Τότε οὖν λα-
ΒΩΝ Ο ΠΙΛΑΤΟΣ ΤΟΝ	-βών ὁ Πιλᾶτος τον
Ι Ν ΕΜΑΣΤΙΓΩΣΕΝ	'Ι(ησοῦ)ν ἐμαστιγωσεν
ΚΑΙ ΟΙ ΣΤΡΑΤΙΩΤΑΙ	και οἱ στρατιωται

29. Upper- and lower-case transcription of John 18:38-40;
19:1.

78

Plate 30

30. Last page of the Fourth Gospel in the Codex Sinaiticus (British Museum); John 21:1-25.

Plate 31 79

ΙΩΑΝΝΗΝ

Ιωανν 21, 1-25

31. Tischendorf's transcription of this page.

32. Codex Ephraemi Rescriptus (Paris, Bibliothèque Nationale, no. 9). The last two lines of the text of St. Ephraem are transcribed at the bottom of the next plate.

33. Transcription of the Gospel text in the Codex Ephraemi Rescriptus; a horizontal line above letters indicates abbreviations of the divine names; a very good magnifying glass is needed to discern the original uncial text under the twelfth-century text.

Plate 33　　　　　　　　81
ΚΑΤΑ ΙΩΑΝΝΗΝ .　1　8　　(17-36)

Λέγει οὖν τῷ Πέτρῳ ἡ παιδίσκη ἡ θυρωρός , Μη καὶ
συ ἐκ τῶν μαθητῶν εἶ τοῦ ἀν(θρώπ)ου τούτου ;
λέγει ἐκεῖνος , Οὐκ εἰμί . εἰστήκεισαν δε οἱ δοῦλοι καὶ οἱ
ὑπηρέται ἀνθρακιαν πεποιη κότες , ὅτι ψῦχος ἦν καὶ
ἐθερμαίνοντο , ἦν δε καὶ ὁ Πέτρος μετ'αὐτῶν ἐστως
καὶ θερμαινόμενος . Ὁ οὖν ἀρχιερευς ἠρώτησεν τον
Ἰ(ησοῦ)ν περι τῶν μαθητῶν αὐτοῦ καὶ περι τῆς διδαχῆς αὐτοῦ.
Ἀπεκρίθη ὁ Ἰ(ησοῦ)ς , Ἐγω παρρησίᾳ λελάληκα τῷ κόσμῳ ,ἐγω
πάντοτε ἐδίδαξα ἐν συναγωγῇ καὶ ἐν τῷ ἱερῷ ὅπου
πάντες οἱ Ἰουδαῖοι συνέρχονται καὶ ἐν κρυπτῷ ἐλά-
-λησα οὐδέν . Τί με ἐρωτᾷς ; ἐρώτησον τους ἀκηκοό-
-τας τί ἐλάλησα αὐτοις . ἴδε οὗτοι οἴδασιν ἃ εἶπον ἐγώ.
ταῦτα δε αὐτοῦ εἰπόντος , εἷς τῶν παρεστώτων ὑπη-
-ρετῶν ἔδωκεν ῥάπισμα τῷ Ἰ(ησο)ῦ εἰπών , Οὕτως ἀποκρί-
-νη τῷ ἀρχιερεῖ ; ἀπεκρίθη αὐτῷ Ἰ(ησοῦ)ς , εἰ κακῶς ἐλάλησα
μαρτύρησον περι τοῦ κακοῦ , εἰ δε καλῶς , τί με δέρεις ;
ἀπέστειλεν οὖν αὐτον ὁ Ἅννας δεδεμένον προς Καϊά-
-φαν τον ἀρχιερέα . ἦν δε Σίμων Πέτρος ἐστως καὶ θερ-
-μαινόμενός . εἶπον οὖν αὐτῷ ,μη καὶ συ ἐκ τῶν μα-
-θητῶν εἶ ἐκείνου . ἠρνήσατο ἐκεῖνος καὶ εἶπεν , Οὐκ εἰ-
-μι. λέγει εἷς ἐκ τῶν δούλων τοῦ ἀρχιερέως , συγγενης
ὢν οὗ ἀπέκοψεν Πέτρος το ὠτίον , οὐκ ἐγώ σε ἴδον
ἐν τῷ κήπῳ μετ'αὐτοῦ ;
Πάλιν οὖν ἠρνήσατο Πέτρος καὶ εὐθέως ἀλέκτωρ ἐφώ-
-νησεν . Ἄγουσιν οὖν τον Ἰ(ησοῦ)ν ἀπο τοῦ Καϊάφα εἰς το πραι-
-τώριον . ἦν δε πρωΐ .καὶ αὐτοι οὐκ εἰσῆλθον εἰς το πραι-
-τώριον , ἵνα μη μιανθῶσιν ἀλλα φάγωσι το πάσχα .
Ἐξῆλθεν οὖν ὁ Πειλᾶτος ἔξω προς αὐτους . καὶ φησίν , Τί-
-να κατηγορίαν φέρετε κατα τοῦ ἀν(θρώπ)ου τούτου ; ἀπεκρίθησαν
καὶ εἶπαν αὐτῷ , εἰ μη ἦν οὗτος κακοποιῶν οὐκ ἄν σοι παρε-
-δώκαμεν αὐτόν . εἶπεν οὖν αὐτοῖς Πειλᾶτος . λάβετε αὐτον
ὑμεις καὶ κατα τον νόμον ὑμῶν κρίνατε αὐτόν .
εἶπον αὐτῷ οἱ Ἰουδαῖοι , Ἡμῖν οὐκ ἔξεστιν ἀποκτεῖναι οὐδέ-
-να , ἵνα ὁ λόγος τοῦ Ἰ(ησο)ῦ πληρωθῇ ὅν εἶπεν σημαίνων ποί-
-ῳ θανάτῳ ἤμελλεν ἀποθνήσκειν .
Εἰσῆλθεν οὖν πάλιν εἰς το πραιτώριον ὁ Πειλᾶτος καὶ ἐφώνη-
-σεν τον Ἰ(ησοῦ)ν καὶ εἶπεν αὐτῷ , Συ εἶ ὁ βασιλευς τῶν Ἰουδαίων ;
ἀπεκρίθη ὁ Ἰ(ησοῦ)ς , Ἀφ'ἑαυτοῦ συ τοῦτο λέγεις ἤ ἄλλοι εἶπον σοι
περι ἐμοῦ ; ἀπεκρίθη ὁ Πειλᾶτος , Μήτι ἐγω Ἰουδαῖός εἰμι ; το
ἔθνος το σον καὶ οἱ ἀρχιερεῖς παρέδωκαν σε ἐμοί . Τί ἐποίησας;
ἀπεκρίθη Ἰ(ησοῦ)ς , Ἡ βασιλεία ἡ ἐμη οὐκ ἔστιν ἐκ τοῦ κόσμου τού-
　　　　　　　　　　　　　　　　　　　　　(του)

-τερον καὶ το πένθος τῆς　　　　καὶ ἡ ἐμη συνείδησις

34. Codex Alexandrinus (London); fifth century. One of the finest manuscripts in the British Museum.

35. Upper-case transcription of the first column (John 18:25-37); lower-case transcription of the second column (John 18:37-40; 19:1-10).

Plate 35   83

1.

ΗΡΝΗΣΑΤΟ ΕΚΕΙΝΟΣ ΚΑΙ ΛΕΓΕΙ
ΟΥΚ ΕΙΜΙ ΛΕΓΕΙ ΕΙΣ ΕΚ ΤΩΝ ΔΟΥ
ΛΩΝ ΤΟΥΑΡΧΙΕΡΕΩΣ ΣΥΓΓΕΝΗΣ
ΩΝ ΟΥ ΑΠΕΚΟΨΕΝ ΠΕΤΡΟΣ ΤΟ
ΩΤΙΟΝ ΟΥΚ ΕΓΩ ΣΕ ΕΙΔΟΝ ΕΝ
ΤΩ ΚΗΠΩ ΜΕΤ ΑΥΤΟΥ ;
ΠΑΛΙΝ ΟΥΝ ΗΡΝΗΣΑΤΟ ΠΕΤΡΟΣ
ΚΑΙ ΕΥΘΕΩΣ ΑΛΕΚΤΩΡ ΕΦΩΝΗ
ΣΕΝ .ΑΓΟΥΣΙΝ ΟΥΝ ΤΟΝ Ι Ν ΑΠΟ
ΤΟΥ ΚΑΙΑΦΑ ΕΙΣ ΤΟ ΠΡΑΙΤΩΡΙΟΝ
ΗΝ ΔΕ ΠΡΩΙ ΚΑΙ ΑΥΤΟΙ ΟΥΚ
ΕΙΣΗΛΘΟΝ ΕΙΣ ΤΟ ΠΡΑΙΤΩΡΙΟΝ ΙΝΑ
ΜΗ ΜΙΑΝΘΩΣΙΝ ΑΛΛΑ ΦΑΓΩΣΙΝ
ΤΟ ΠΑΣΧΑ ΕΞΗΛΘΕΝ ΟΥΝ Ο ΠΕΙΛΑ
ΤΟΣ ΠΡΟΣ ΑΥΤΟΥΣ ΚΑΙ ΕΙΠΕΝ
ΤΙΝΑ ΚΑΤΗΓΟΡΙΑΝ ΦΕΡΕΤΕ ΚΑΤΑ
ΤΟΥ ΑΝ(ΘΡΩΠ)ΟΥ ΤΟΥΤΟΥ ;ΑΠΕΚΡΙΘΗΣΑΝ
ΚΑΙ ΕΙΠΟΝ ΑΥΤΩ ΕΙ ΜΗ ΗΝ ΟΥΤΟΣ
ΚΑΚΟΠΟΙΟΣ ΟΥΚ ΑΝ ΣΟΙ ΠΑΡΕΔΩ
ΚΑΜΕΝ ΑΥΤΟΝ ΕΙΠΕΝ ΟΥΝ ΑΥΤΟΙΣ
Ο ΠΕΙΛΑΤΟΣ ΛΑΒΕΤΕ ΑΥΤΟΝ ΥΜΕΙΣ
ΚΑΙ ΚΑΤΑ ΤΟΝ ΝΟΜΟΝ ΥΜΩΝ ΚΡΙ
ΝΑΤΕ ΑΥΤΟΝ . ΕΙΠΟΝ ΔΕ ΑΥΤΩ
ΟΙ ΙΟΥΔΑΙΟΙ ΗΜΙΝ ΟΥΚ ΕΞΕΣΤΙΝ
ΑΠΟΚΤΕΙΝΑΙ ΟΥΔΕΝΑ ΙΝΑ Ο ΛΟΓΟΣ
ΤΟΥ ΙΥ ΠΛΗΡΩΘΗ ΟΝ ΕΙΠΕΝ ΣΗ
ΜΑΙΝΩΝ ΠΟΙΩ ΘΑΝΑΤΩ ΗΜΕΛΛΕΝ
ΑΠΟΘΝΗΣΚΕΙΝ   ΕΙΣΗΛΘΕΝ
ΟΥΝ ΕΙΣ ΤΟ ΠΡΑΙΤΩΡΙΟΝ ΠΑΛΙΝ
Ο ΠΕΙΛΑΤΟΣ ΚΑΙ ΕΦΩΝΗΣΕΝ ΤΟΝ
ΙΝ ΚΑΙ ΕΙΠΕΝ ΑΥΤΟΙΣ ΣΥ ΕΙ Ο ΒΑΣΙ
ΛΕΥΣ ΤΩΝ ΙΟΥΔΑΙΩΝ ;
ΑΠΕΚΡΙΝΑΤΟ Ο ΙΣ ΑΦ ΕΑΥΤΟΥ ΣΥ ΤΟΥ
ΤΟ ΛΕΓΕΙΣ Η ΑΛΛΟΙ ΣΟΙ ΕΙΠΟΝ ΠΕ
ΡΙ ΕΜΟΥ ; ΑΠΕΚΡΙΘΗ Ο ΠΕΙΛΑΤΟΣ
ΜΗΤΙ ΕΓΩ ΙΟΥΔΑΙΟΣ ΕΙΜΙ ΤΟ Ε
ΘΝΟΣ ΤΟ ΣΟΝ ΚΑΙ ΟΙ ΑΡΧΙΕΡΕΙΣ
ΠΑΡΕΔΩΚΑΝ ΣΕ ΕΜΟΙ ΤΙ ΕΠΟΙΗΣΑΣ ;
ΑΠΕΚΡΙΘΗ Ο ΙΣ Η ΒΑΣΙΛΕΙΑ Η ΕΜΗ
ΟΥΚ ΕΣΤΙΝ ΕΚ ΤΟΥ ΚΟΣΜΟΥ ΤΟΥΤΟΥ
ΕΙ ΕΚ ΤΟΥ ΚΟΣΜΟΥ ΤΟΥΤΟΥ ΗΝ
Η ΒΑΣΙΛΕΙΑ Η ΕΜΗ ΟΙ ΥΠΗΡΕΤΑΙ ΑΝ
ΟΙ ΕΜΟΙ ΗΓΩΝΙΖΟΝΤΟ ΙΝΑ ΜΗ
ΠΑΡΑΔΟΘΩ ΤΟΙΣ ΙΟΥΔΑΙΟΙΣ ΝΥΝ
ΔΕ Η ΒΑΣΙΛΕΙΑ Η ΕΜΗ ΟΥΚ ΕΣΤΙΝ
ΕΝΤΕΥΘΕΝ ΕΙΠΕΝ ΟΥΝ ΑΥΤΩ
Ο ΠΕΙΛΑΤΟΣ : ΟΥΚΟΥΝ ΒΑΣΙΛΕΥΣ ΕΙ ΣΥ
ΑΠΕΚΡΙΘΗ Ο ΙΣ ΣΥ ΛΕΓΕΙΣ ΟΤΙ ΒΑ
ΣΙΛΕΥΣ ΕΙΜΙ ΕΓΩ
ΕΓΩ ΕΙΣ ΤΟΥΤΟ ΚΑΙ ΓΕΓΕΝΝΗΜΑΙ
ΚΑΙ ΕΙΣ ΤΟΥΤΟ ΕΛΗΛΥΘΑ ΕΙΣ ΤΟΝ

2.

κόσμον, ἵνα μαρτυρήσω
ἀληθείᾳ. πᾶς ὁ ὢν ἐκ τῆς ἀλη-
-θείας ἀκούει μου τῆς φωνῆς.
λέγει αὐτῷ ὁ Πιλᾶτος ,Τί ἐστιν
ἀλήθεια ; καὶ τοῦτο εἰπὼν πά-
-λιν ἐξῆλθεν προς τους Ἰουδαίους,
καὶ λέγει αὐτοῖς ,Ἐγὼ οὐδεμίαν
αἰτίαν εὑρίσκω ἐν αὐτῷ .
Ἔστιν δε συνήθεια ὑμῖν ἵνα ἕνα
ὑμῖν ἀπολύσω ἐν τῷ πάσχα , βούλε-
-σθαι οὖν ἀπολύσω ὑμῖν τον βασιλέα
τῶν Ἰουδαίων ; ἐκραύγασαν οὖν
πάλιν πάντες λέγοντες , μη τοῦ-
-τον ἀλλα τον βαραββᾶν . ἦν δε ὁ βα-
-ραββᾶς λῃστής .19.Τότε οὖν ἔλαβεν
ὁ Πειλᾶτος τον ἸΝ καὶ ἐμαστίγω-
-σεν καὶ οἱ στρατιῶται πλέξαν-
-τες στέφανον ἐξ ἀκανθῶν
ἐπέθηκαν αὐτοῦ ἐπι την κεφαλην
καὶ εἱμάτιον πορφυροῦν περι-
-έβαλον αὐτόν καὶ ἔλεγον : Χαῖρε
ὁ βασιλευς τῶν Ἰουδαίων καὶ
ἐδίδουν αὐτῷ ῥαπίσματα
καὶ ἐξῆλθεν πάλιν ἔξω ὁ Πειλᾶ-
-τος καὶ λέγει αὐτοῖς ,Ἴδε ἄγω ὑμῖν
αὐτον ἔξω ἵνα γνῶτε ὅτι οὐ-
-δεμίαν ἐν αὐτῷ αἰτίαν εὑρί-
-σκω. ἐξῆλθεν οὖν ὁ ἸΣ ἔξω
φορῶν τον ἀκάνθινον στεφα-
-νον καὶ το πορφυροῦν ἱμάτιον
καὶ λέγει αὐτοῖς Ἴδε ὁ ἄν(θρωπ)ος.
ὅτε οὖν ἴδον αὐτον οἱ ἀρχιερεῖς
καὶ οἱ ὑπηρέται ἐκραύγασαν λέ-
-γοντες, Σταύρωσον σταύρω-
-σον αὐτον . λέγει αὐτοῖς
ὁ Πειλᾶτος λάβετε αὐτον ὑμεῖς
καὶ σταυρώσατε, ἐγω γαρ
οὐχ εὑρίσκω ἐν αὐτῷ αἰτίαν ,
ἀπεκρίθησαν αὐτῷ οἱ Ἰουδαῖοι
Ἡμεῖς νόμον ἔχομεν , καὶ κα-
-τα τον νόμον ἡμῶν ὀφίλει(ε)
ἀποθανεῖν ὅτι ἑαυτον υιον Θ(εο)ῦ
ἐποίησεν . ὅτε οὖν ἤκουσεν
ὁ Πειλᾶτος τοῦτον τον λόγον
μᾶλλον ἐφοβήθη καὶ εἰσῆλ -
-θεν εἰς το πραιτώριον πάλιν
καὶ λέγει τῷ ἸΥ ,Πόθεν εἶ σύ ;
ὁ δε ἸΣ ἀπόκρισιν οὐκ ἔδωκεν
αὐτῷ .λέγει αὐτῷ ὁ Πειλᾶτος
Ἐμοι οὐ λαλεῖς ; οὐκ οἶδας ὅτι
ἐξουσίαν ἔχω ἀπολῦσαι σε

ΗΡΝΗСΑΤΟ ЄΚЄΙΝΟС ΚΑΙ ЄΙΠЄΝ · ΟΥΚЄΙΜΙ · ΛЄΓЄΙ ЄС ЄΚ ΤΩΝ ΔΟΛΩΝ
ΤΟΥ ΑΡΧΙЄΡЄΩС · СΥΝ ΓЄΝΗС ΩΝ ΟΥ ΑΠЄΚΟΨЄΝ ΠЄΤΡΟС ΤΟ ΩΤ · ΗΝ
ΟΥΚ ЄΤΩ СΑΛΟΝ ЄΝ ΤΩ ΚΗΠΩ ΜЄΤ ΑΥΤΟΥ ·
ΠΑΛΙΝ ΟΥΝ ΗΡΝΗСΑΤΟ ΠЄΤΡΩС · ΚΑΙ ЄΥΘЄΩС ΑΛЄΚΤΩΡ ЄΦΩΝΗСЄΝ ·
ΑΓΟΥСΙΝ ΟΥΝ ΤΟΝ ΙΝ ΑΠΟ ΤΟΥ ΚΑΙΦΑ ЄΙС ΤΟ ΠΡΑΙΤΩΡΙΟΝ ·
ΗΝ ΔЄ ΠΡΩΙ · ΚΑΙ ΑΥΤΟΙ ΟΥΚ ЄΙСΗΛΘΟΝ ЄΙС ΤΟ ΠΡΑΙΤΩΡΙΟΝ
ΙΝΑ ΜΗ ΜΙΑΝΘΩСΙΝ · ΑΛΛΑ ΦΑΤΩСΙΝ ΤΟ ΠΑСΧΑ ·
ЄΞΗΛΘЄΝ ΟΥΝ Ο ΠΙΛΑΤΟС ΠΡΟС ΑΥΤΟΥС · ΚΑΙ ЄΙΠЄΝ ·
ΤΙΝΑ ΚΑΤΗΓΟΡΙΑΝ ΦЄΡЄΤΑΙ ΚΑΤΑ ΤΟΥ ΑΝΟΥ ΤΟΥΤΟΥ ·
ΑΠЄΚΡΙΘΗСΑΝ ΚΑΙ ЄΙΠЄΝ ΑΥΤΩ · ЄΙ ΜΗ ΗΝ ΟΥΤΟС
ΚΑΚΟΠΟΙΟС · ΟΥΚ ΑΝ СΟΙ ΠΑΡЄΔΩΚΑΜЄΝ ΑΥΤΟΝ ·
ЄΙΠЄΝ ΟΥΝ ΑΥΤΟΙС Ο ΠЄΙΛΑΤΟС · ΛΑΒЄΤΑΙ ΑΥΤΟΝ ΥΜЄΙС ·
ΚΑΙ ΚΑΤΑ ΤΟΝ ΝΟΜΟΝ ΥΜΩΝ ΚΡΙΝΑΤЄ ΑΥΤΟΝ ·
ЄΙΠΟΝ ΔЄ ΑΥΤΩ ΟΙ ΙΟΥΔΑΙΟΙ · ΗΜΙΝ ΟΥΚ ЄΞЄСΤΙΝ
ΑΠΟΚΤЄΙΝΑΙ ΟΥΔЄΝΑ · ΙΝΑ Ο ΛΟΓΟС ΤΟΥ ΙΥ ΠΛΗΡΩΘΗ
ΟΝ ЄΙΠЄΝ · СΗΜΙΝΩΝ ΠΟΙΩ ΘΑΝΑΤΩ ΗΜЄΛΛЄΝ ΑΠΟΘΝΗСΚЄΙΝ
ЄΙСΗΛΘΟΝ ΟΥΝ ΠΑΛΙΝ ЄΙС ΤΟ ΠΡΑΙΤΩΡΙΟΝ ΠЄΙΛΑΤΟС ·
ΚΑΙ ЄΦΩΝΗСЄΝ ΤΟΝ ΙΝ · ΚΑΙ ЄΙΠЄΝ ΑΥΤΩ ·
СΥ ЄΙ Ο ΒΑСΙΛЄΥС ΤΩΝ ΙΟΥΔΑΙΩΝ · ΚΑΙ ΑΠЄΚΡΙΝΑΤΟ ΟΙС ·
ΑΦЄ ΑΥΤΟΥ ΤΟΥΤΟ ΛЄΓЄΙС · Η ΑΛΛΟΙ
ЄΠΟΝ СΟΙ ΠЄΡΙ ЄΜΟΥ · ΑΠЄΚΡΙΘΗ Ο ΠЄΙΛΑΤΟС · ΜΗΤΙ ЄΓΩ
ΙΟΥΔΑΙΟС ЄΙΜΙ · ΤΟ ЄΘΝΟС ΤΟ СΟΝ ΚΑΙ ΑΡΧΙЄΡЄΙС ·
ΠΑΡЄΔΩΚΑΝ СЄ ЄΜΟΙ · ΤΙ ЄΠΟΙΗСΑС · ΑΠЄΚΡΙΘΗ ΙС ·
Η ΒΑСΙΛЄΙΑ Η ЄΜΗ · ΟΥΚ ЄСΤΙΝ ЄΚ ΤΟΥ ΚΟСΜΟΥ ΤΟΥΤΟΥ ·
ЄΙ ЄΚ ΤΟΥ ΚΟСΜΟΥ ΤΟΥΤΟΥ ΗΝ Η ЄΜΗ ΒΑСΙΛЄΙΑ ·
ΟΙ ΥΠΗΡЄΤΑΙ ΑΝΟΙ ЄΜΟΙ ΗΓΩΝΙΖΟΤΟ ΙΝΑ ΜΗ ΠΑΡΑΔΩ ΤΟΙС ·
ΙΟΥΔΑΙС · ΝΥΝ ΔЄ Η ΒΑСΙΛЄΙΑ Η ЄΜΗ ΟΥΚ ЄСΤΙΝ ЄΝΤЄΥΘЄΝ ·
ЄΙΠЄΝ ΟΥΝ ΑΥΤΩ Ο ΠЄΙΛΑΤΟС · ΟΥΚΟΥΝ ΒΑСΙΛЄΥС ЄΙ СΥ ·
ΑΠЄΚΡΙΘΗ ΟΙС · СΥ ΛЄΓЄΙС ΟΤΙ ΒΑСΙΛЄΥС ЄΙΜΙ ·
ЄΓΩ ЄΙС ΤΟΥΤΟ ΓЄΓЄΝΝΗΜΑΙ · ΚΑΙ ЄΙС ΤΟΥΤΟ ЄΛΗΛΥΘΑ
ЄΙС ΤΟΝ ΚΟСΜΟΝ · ΙΝΑ ΜΑΡΤΥΡΗСΩ ΤΗ ΑΛΗΘЄΙΑ ·
ΠΑС Ο ΩΝ ЄΚ ΤΗС ΑΛΗΘЄΙΑС · ΑΚΟΥΙ ΜΟΥ ΤΗС ΦΩΝΗС ·
ΛЄΓЄΙ ΑΥΤΩ Ο ΠЄΙΛΑΤΟС · ΤΙ ЄСΤΙΝ ΑΛΗΘЄΙΑ ·

36. Codex Bezae (Cambridge). Bilingual (Latin and Greek) manuscript; shown here is the Greek for John 18:25-38.

37. Transcription of this page. Sacred names are abbreviated in the Codex, filled out (in parentheses) in the transcription.

Plate 37　　　　　　　85

ΚΑΤΑ ΙΩΑΝΝΗΝ . 1 8　(25-38)

Ἠρνήσατο ἐκεῖνος και εἶπεν , Οὐκ εἰμι .λέγει εἷς ἐκ τῶν δο(ύ)λων
τοῦ ἀρχιερέως , συνγενης ὤν οὗ ἀπέκοψεν Πέτρος το ὠτίον,
Οὐκ ἐγώ σε ἴδον ἐν τῷ κήπῳ μετ' αὐτοῦ ;
πάλιν οὖν ἠρνήσατο Πέτρος . και εὐθέως ἀλέκτωρ ἐφώνησεν .
Ἄγουσιν οὖν τον 'Ι(ησοῦ)ν ἀπο τοῦ Καϊφα εἰς το πραιτώριον.
ἦν δε πρωΐ . και αὐτοι οὐκ εἰσῆλθον εἰς το πραιτώριον ,
ἵνα μη μιανθῶσιν ἀλλα φάγωσιν το πάσχα .
ἐξῆλθεν οὖν ὁ Πιλατος προς αὐτους και εἶπεν ,
Τίνα κατηγορίαν φέρεται κατα τοῦ ἀν(θρώπ)ου τούτου ;
ἀπεκρίθησαν και εἶπεν αὐτῷ , Εἰ μη ἦν οὗτος
κακοποιός , οὐκ ἄν σοι παρεδώκαμεν αὐτόν .
εἶπεν οὖν αὐτοῖς ὁ Πειλᾶτος , Λάβεται αὐτον ὑμεῖς ,
και κατα τον νόμον ὑμῶν κρίνατε αὐτόν .
εἶπον δε αὐτῷ οἱ 'Ιουδαῖοι , Ἡμῖν οὐκ ἔξεστιν
ἀποκτεῖναι οὐδένα ἵνα ὁ λόγος τοῦ 'Ι(ησο)ῦ πληρωθῇ
ὃν εἶπεν σημαίνων ποίῳ θανάτῳ ἤμελλεν ἀποθνήσκειν .
'Εισῆλθον οὖν πάλιν εἰς το πραιτώριον Πειλᾶτος
και ἐφώνησεν τον 'Ι(ησοῦ)ν και εἶπεν αὐτῷ
Συ εἶ ὁ βασιλευς τῶν 'Ιουδαίων ; και ἀπεκρίνατο ὁ 'Ι(ησοῦ)ς
'Αφ' ἑαυτοῦ τοῦτο λέγεις ἤ ἄλλοι
εἶπον σοι περι ἐμοῦ ; ἀπεκρίθη ὁ Πειλᾶτος , Μήτι ἐγω
'Ιουδαῖός εἰμι ; το ἔθνος το σον και ἀρχιερεῖς
παρέδωκαν σε ἐμοί . Τί ἐποίησας ; ἀπεκρίθη 'Ι(ησοῦ)ς
ἡ βασιλεία ἡ ἐμη οὐκ ἔστιν ἐκ τοῦ κόσμου τούτου .
εἰ ἐκ τοῦ κόσμου τούτου ἦν ἡ ἐμη βασιλεία
οἱ ὑπηρέται ἄν οἱ ἐμοι ἠγωνίζοντο ἵνα μη παραδ(οθ)ῶ τοῖς
'Ιουδαῖ(οι)ς , νῦν.δε ἡ βασιλεία ἡ ἐμη οὐκ ἔστιν ἐντεῦθεν .
εἶπεν οὖν αὐτῷ ὁ Πειλᾶτος , Οὐκοῦν βασιλευς εἶ σύ ;
ἀπεκρίθη ὁ 'Ι(ησου)ς , Συ λέγεις ὅτι βασιλεύς εἰμι .
ἐγω εἰς τοῦτο γεγέννημαι και εἰς τοῦτο ἐλήλυθα
εἰς τόν κόσμον ἵνα μαρτυρήσω(ν) τῇ ἀληθείᾳ
πᾶς ὁ ὤν ἐκ τῆς ἀληθείας ἀκού(ε)ι μου τῆς φωνῆς .
λέγει αὐτῷ ὁ Πειλᾶτος , Τί ἐστιν ἀλήθεια ;

38. A page of the Freer Codex (Washington); John 4:53–5:11.

Plate 39   87

4 (53)   - 5 (11)

τῇ ὥρᾳ ἐν ᾗ εἶπεν αὐτῷ ὁ ΙΣ , ὁ υἱός σου ζῇ
καὶ ἐπίστευσεν αὐτὸς καὶ ἡ οἰκία αὐτοῦ ὅλη.
Τοῦτο δε πάλιν β ἐποίησεν σημεῖον ὁ Ι Σ ἐλθων
ἐκ τῆς Ἰουδέας εἰς την Γαλιλαίαν .Μετα
ταῦτα ἦν ἑορτη τῶν Ἰουδέων ,καὶ ἀνέβη
Ι Σ εἰς 'ιεροσόλυμα. ἔστιν δε ἐν τοῖς 'ιεροσολύ-
-μοις ἐπι τῇ προβατικῇ κολυμβήθρα τη ἐ-
-πιλεγομένη Ἐβραϊστι Βηθζαθά, ε στοας ἔχουσα.
ἐν ταύταις κατέκιτο πλῆθος τῶν ἀσθενούντων,
τυφγῶν, χωλῶν, ξηρῶν, ἐκδεχομένοι την τοῦ
ὕδατος κίνησιν . ἦν δε τις ἅνος ἐκι μ κ η ἔτη
ἔχων ἐν τῇ ἀσθενία αὐτοῦ . τοῦτον εἰδων
ὁ ΙΣ κατακίμενον, καὶ γνους ὅτι πολυν ἤδη
χρόνον ἔχι , λέγι αὐτῷ .Θέλις ὑγιης γενέσ-
-θαι ; ἀπεκρίθη αὐτῷ ὁ ἀσθενων,
ΚΕ , ἄν(θρωπ)ον οὐκ ἔχω ἵνα ὅταν ταραχθῇ
το ὕδωρ βάλῃ με εἰς την κολυμβή-
-θραν . ἐν(ος) δε ᾧ ἔρχομε ἐγω ,ἄλλος
προ ἐμοῦ καταβένι .
λέγι αὐτῷ ὁ ΙΣ , ἔγιρε ἆρον τον
κράβαττόν σου καὶ περιπάτι
καὶ ἐγένετο ὑγιης ὁ ἄν(θρωπ)ος καὶ ἦ-
,-ρεν τον κράβαττον αὐτοῦ καὶ
περιέπατι .
⁷Ἦν δε σάββατον ἐν ἐκίνη τῇ
ἡμέρᾳ .
Ἔλεγον οὖν οἱ Ἰουδέοι τῷ τεθεραπευ-
-μένῳ ,Σάββατόν ἐστιν , καὶ
οὐκ ἔξεστιν σοι ἆραι τον κράβαττόν σου
ὁ δε ἀπεκρίνατο αὐτοῖς , ὁ ποι(ή)σας
με ὑγιην , ἐκῖνός μοι εἶπεν , ⁷Ἆρον τον
       (κράβαττόν σου)

39. Lower-case transcription to facilitate the reading of the original.

40. Caesarea Codex (Leningrad).

Plate 41

89

ΚΑΤΑ ΙΩΑΝΝΗΝ. 7 (35-39)

ΕΛΛΗΝΩΝ ΜΕΛ	Ἑλλήνων μέλ–
ΛΕΙ ΠΟΡΕΥΕΣ	–λει πορεύεσ–
ΘΕ ΚΑΙ ΔΙΔΑΣΚΕΙΝ	–θε καὶ διδάσκειν
ΤΟΥΣ ΕΛΛΗΝΑΣ	τοὺς Ἕλληνας .
ΤΙΣ ΕΣΤΙΝ Ο ΛΟ	Τίς ἐστιν ὁ λό–
ΓΟΣ ΟΥΤΟΣ ΟΝ	–γος οὗτος ὅν
ΕΙΠΕΝ ΖΗΤΗ	εἶπεν : ζητή–
ΣΕΤΕ ΜΕ ΚΑΙ ΟΥΧ	–σετε με καὶ οὐχ
ΕΥΡΗΣΕΤΕ ΚΑΙ	εὑρήσετε , καὶ
ΟΠΟΥ ΕΙΜΙ Ε	ὅπου εἰμι ἐ–
ΓΩ ΥΜΙΣ ΟΥ ΔΥ	–γω ὑμις οὐ δύ–
ΝΑΣΘΕ ΕΛΘΕΙΝ	–νασθε ἐλθεῖν .
ΕΝ ΔΕ ΤΗ ΕΣΧΑ	Ἐν δε τῇ ἐσχά–
ΤΗ ΗΜΕΡΑ ΤΗ ΜΕ	–τη ἡμέρᾳ τῇ με–
ΓΑΛΗ ΤΗΣ ΕΟΡ	–γάλη τῆς ἑορ– .
ΤΗΣ ΕΙΣΤΗΚΕΙ	–τῆς εἰστήκει
Ο ΙΣ ΚΑΙ ΕΚΡΑ	ὁ Ἰ(ησοῦ)ς καὶ ἔκρα–
ΞΕΝ ΛΕΓΩΝ ΕΑΝ	–ξεν λέγων : Ἐάν
ΤΙΣ ΔΙΨΑ ΕΡΧΕΣ	τις διψᾷ, ἐρχέσ–
ΘΩ ΠΡΟΣ ΜΕ	–θω πρός με,
ΚΑΙ ΠΙΝΕΤΩ	καὶ πινέτω .
Ο ΠΙΣΤΕΥΩΝ ΕΙΣ	ὁ πιστεύων εἰς
ΕΜΕ ΚΑΘΩΣ ΕΙ	ἐμέ καθὼς εἶ–
ΠΕΝ Η ΓΡΑΦΗ	–πεν ἡ γραφή ,
ΠΟΤΑΜΟΙ ΕΚ	ποταμοι ἐκ
ΤΗΣ ΚΟΙΛΙΑΣ ΑΥ	τῆς κοιλίας αὐ–
ΤΟΥ ΡΕΥΣΩΣΙ	–τοῦ ῥεύσωσι
ΥΔΑΤΟΣ ΖΩΝΤΟΣ	ὕδατος ζῶντος .
ΤΟΥΤΟ ΔΕ ΕΙΠΕΝ	τοῦτο δε εἶπεν
ΠΕΡΙ ΤΟΥ ΠΝΣ	περι τοῦ Πν(εύματο)ς
ΟΥ ΕΜΕΛΛΟΝ	οὗ ἔμελλον
ΛΑΜΒΑΝΕΙΝ ΟΙ	λαμβάνειν οἱ
	(πιστεύσαντες εἰς αὐτόν)

41. Transcription in upper-case and lower-case letters; John 7:35-
39.

42. Codex Koridethi (Tiflis Gr. 28), written in crude and irregular capitals; John 9:17-26.

Plate 43 91

KOPIΔEΘI .

KATA IΩANNHN   9   (17-26)

(τί συ λέγεις περι αὐτοῦ)
ὅτι ἠνέῳξέν σοὐ το-
-υς ὀφθαλμούς ;
ὁ δε εἶπεν ὅτι Προ-
-φήτης ἐστίν .
Οὐκ ἐπίστευον δε
οἱ Ἰουδαῖοι περι αὐτοῦ
ὅτι ἦν τυφλος και ἀ-
-νέβλεψεν ἔως ὅ-
-του ἐφώνησαν
τους γονεῖς αὐτοῦ
τοῦ ἀναβλέψαντος
και ἠρώτησαν αὐτο-
-υς λέγοντες , Οὗτ-
-ός ἐστιν ὁ υἱός ὑμῶν ,
ὅν ὑμεῖς ἐλέγετε
ὅτι τυφλος ἐγενν-
-ήθη ; πῶς οὖν βλέπει ἄρτι;
ἀπεκρίθησαν αὐτοῖς
οἱ γονεῖς αὐτοῦ και
εἶπον , Οἴδαμεν ὅ-
-τι οὗτός ἐστιν ὁ υἱ-
-ός ἡμῶν και ὅτι τυ-
-φλος ἐγεννήθη , Π-
-ῶς δε νῦν βλέπει οὐ-
-κ(υ) οἴδαμεν ,ἤ τίς αὐτο-
-ῦ ἀνέῳξεν τους ὀ-
-φθαλμους ἡμεῖς
οὐκ οἴδαμεν . αὐτον
ἐρωτήσατε ,ἡλικεί-
-αν ἔχει , αὐτος περι

ἑαυτοῦ λαλήσει .
ταῦτα εἶπον οἱ γονεῖ-
-ς αὐτοῦ ὅτι ἐφοβ-
-οῦντο τους Ἰουδ-
-αίους ,ἤδη γαρ συν-
-ετίθειντο οἱ Ἰου-
-δε(αῖ)οι ἵνα ἐάν τις α-
-ὐτον ὁμολογεί-
-σει Χ(ριστό·)ν ἀποσυνά-
-γωγος γένηται .
δια τοῦτο οἱ γον-
-εῖς αὐτοῦ εἶπον
ὅτι Ἡλικίαν ἔχει,
αὐτον ἐρωτίσαται .
Ἐφώνησαν οὖν τον
ἄν(θρωπ)ον ἐκ δευτέρ-
-ου ὅς ἦν τυφλος
και εἶπαν αὐτῷ , Δ-
-ος δόξαν τω Θ(ε)ῷ .
ἡμεῖς οἴδαμεν
ὅτι οὗτος ὁ ἄν(θρωπ)ος
ἁμαρτωλός ἐστιν .
εἶπεν οὖν ἐκεῖνο-
-ς , Εἰ ἁμαρτω(ο)λός
ἐστην οὐκ οἶδα
ἕν οἶδα , ὅτι τυ-
-φλος ὢν ἄρτι β-
-λέπω .
εἶπον οὖν αὐτῷ
πάλιν , Τί ἐποίησεν
σοι ;

43. Lower-case transcription; missing letters are added, and abbreviations filled out, in parentheses.

44. Vienna Codex with marks for reading and singing.

Plate 45   93

ΚΑΤΑ ΙΩΑΝΝΗΝ   7   (13-18)

(Οὐδεις μέντοι)		τοῦ πέμψαν-	ΤΟΥ ΠΕΜΨΑΝ
παρρησία ἐ)	ΠΑΡΡΗΣΙΑ Ε	τός με	ΤΟΣ ΜΕ
-λάλει περι αὑ-	ΛΑΛΕΙ ΠΕΡΙ ΑΥ	ἐάν τις θέλει	ΕΑΝ ΤΙΣ ΘΕΛΕΙ
-τοῦ δια τον	ΤΟΥ ΔΙΑ ΤΟΝ	το θέλημα	ΤΟ ΘΕΛΗΜΑ
φόβον τῶν	ΦΟΒΟΝ ΤΩΝ	αὐτοῦ ποιεῖν	ΑΥΤΟΥ ΠΟΙΕΙΝ
Ἰουδαίων .	ΙΟΥΔΑΙΩΝ·	γνώσεται	ΓΝΩΣΕΤΑΙ
Ἤδη δε	ΗΔΗ ΔΕ	περι τῆς δι-	ΠΕΡΙ ΤΗΣ ΔΙ
τῆς ἑορτῆς·	ΤΗΣ ΕΟΡΤΗΣ	-δαχῆς , πό-	ΔΑΧΗΣ ΠΟ
μεσούσης	ΜΕΣΟΥΣΗΣ	-τερον ἐκ	ΤΕΡΟΝ ΕΚ
ἀνέβη ὁ'Ι(ησοῦ)ς	ΑΝΕΒΗ Ι Σ	τοῦ θ(εο)ῦ ἐστιν	ΤΟΥ ΘΥ ΕΣΤΙΝ
εἰς το ἱερον	ΕΙΣ ΤΟ ΙΕΡΟΝ	ἤ ἐγω ἀπ'ἐ-	Η ΕΓΩ ΑΠΕ
και ἐδίδασκε	ΚΑΙ ΕΔΙΔΑΣΚΕ·	-μαυτοῦ οὐ	ΜΑΥΤΟΥ ΟΥ
και ἐθαύμα-	ΚΑΙ ΕΘΑΥΜΑ	λαλῶ . ὁ ἀφ'ἐ-	ΛΑΛΩ Ο ΑΦ Ε
-ζον οἱ Ἰουδαῖ-	ΖΟΝ ΟΙ ΙΟΥΔΑΙ	-αυτοῦ λαλῶν	ΑΥΤΟΥ ΛΑΛΩΝ
-οι λέγοντες	ΟΙ ΛΕΓΟΝΤΕΣ	την δόξαν	ΤΗΝ ΔΟΞΑΝ
Πῶς οὗτος	ΠΩΣ ΟΥΤΟΣ	την ἰδίαν ζη-	ΤΗΝ ΙΔΙΑΝ ΖΗ
γράμματα οἶδεν	ΓΡΑΜΜΑΤΑ ΟΙΔΕΝ	-τεῖ .	ΤΕΙ
μη μεμαθη-	ΜΗ ΜΕΜΑΘΗ	ὁ δε ζητῶν	Ο ΔΕ ΖΗΤΩΝ
-κώς ;	ΚΩΣ	την δόξαν	ΤΗΝ ΔΟΞΑΝ
ἀπεκρίθη οὖν	ΑΠΕΚΡΙΘΗ ΟΥΝ	τοῦ πέμψαν-	ΤΟΥ ΠΕΜΨΑΝ
αὐτοῖς ὁ 'Ι(ησοῦ)ς	ΑΥΤΟΙΣ Ο Ι Σ	-τος αὐτόν	ΤΟΣ ΑΥΤΟΝ
και εἶπεν	ΚΑΙ ΕΙΠΕΝ	οὗτος ἀλη-	ΟΥΤΟΣ ΑΛΗ
ἡ ἐμη διδαχη	Η ΕΜΗ ΔΙΔΑΧΗ	-θής ἐστιν	ΘΗΣ ΕΣΤΙΝ
οὐκ ἔστιν	ΟΥΚ ΕΣΤΙΝ	και ἀδικία ε-	ΚΑΙ ΑΔΙΚΙΑ Ε
ἐμη ἀλλα	ΕΜΗ ΑΛΛΑ	-ν αὐτῷ	Ν ΑΥΤΩ
		(οὐκ ἔστιν .)	

45. Transcriptions, upper-case and lower-case juxtaposed.

Plate 46

46. Uspenskij Codex, written in 835; Leningrad, No. 219, the first dated minuscule manuscript.

Plate 47   95

17   (8–12)

και ἔγνωσαν ἀληθῶς ὅτι παρα σοῦ
ἐξῆλθον , και ἐπίστευσαν ὅτι σύ
με ἀπέστειλας . ἐγω περι αὐτῶν
ἐρωτῶ . οὐ περι τοῦ κόσμου
ἐρωτῶ , ἀλλα περι ὧν δέδωκά-
-ς μοι ,ὅτι σοί εἰσιν ,και τα ἐμα πάν-
-τα σά ἐστιν και τα σα ἐμά και δεδό-
-ξασμαι ἐν αὐτοῖς . και οὐκέτι
εἰμι ἐν τῷ κόσμῳ , και οὗτοι ἐν
τῷ κόσμῳ εἰσιν , κἀγω προς σε
ἔρχομαι . Πάτερ ἅγιε , τήρη-
-σον αὐτους ἐν τῷ ὀνόματί σου ᾧ
δέδωκάς μοι , ἵνα ὦσιν ἕν κα-
-θως ἡμεῖς . ὅτε ἤμην μετ'αὐ-
-τῶν ἐν τῷ κόσμῳ , ἐγω ἐτήρουν αὐ-
-τους ἐν τῷ ὀνόματί σου οὕς δέ-
-δωκάς μοι ἐφύλαξα , και οὐδεις
ἐξ αὐτῶν ἀπώλετο εἰ μη ὁ υἱος
τῆς ἀπωλείας , ἵνα ἡ γραφη πλη-
-ρωθῇ .

47. Transcription of this specimen so representative of the early
minuscule of the *codices vetustissimi* (from the ninth century to
the beginning of the tenth).

48. Greek Codex no. 70 of Paris. First page with painting of St. John.

Plate 49   97

ΕΥΑΓΓΕ
ΛΙΟΝ   ΚΑΤΑ
ΙΩΑΝΝΗΝ.

'Εν ἀρχῇ ἦν ὁ λόγος , καὶ ὁ λόγος

ἦν προς τον Θ(εὸ)ν, και Θ(εο)ς ἦν ὁ λό-

-γος . οὗτος ἦν ἐν ἀρχῇ προς τον

Θ(εὸ)ν .πάντα δι'αὐτοῦ ἐγένετο , και

χωρις αὐτοῦ ἐγένετο οὐδε ἕν . ὅ

γέγονεν ἐν αὐτῷ ζων ἦν και

ἡ ζων ἦν το φῶς τῶν ἀν(θρωπ)ων και

το φῶς ἐν τῇ σκοτία φαίνει , και

ἡ σκοτία αὐτο οὐ κατέλαβεν .

'Εγένετο   ἄν(θρωπ)ος ἀπεσταλμένος παρα

(παρα Θεοῦ,)

49. Transcription: title upper-case, 1.1-6 lower-case.

μῶν κρίμα τὸ αὐτοῦ· ἔἰπον οὖν
αὐτῷ οἱ ἰουδαῖοι· ἡμῖν οὐκ ἔξεϲτιν
ἀποκτεῖναι οὐδένα· ἵνα ὁ λόγος
τοῦ ιυ πληρωθῇ ὃν εἶπεν. σημαίνων ποίῳ θανάτῳ ἔμελλεν ἀπο-
θνήϲκειν· Εἰσῆλθεν οὖν εἰς τὸ
πραιτώριον πάλιν ὁ πιλᾶτος· ἐ-
φώνησεν τὸν ιν καὶ εἶπεν αὐτῷ·
σὺ εἶ ὁ βασιλεὺς τῶν ἰουδαίων;
ἀπεκρίθη αὐτῷ ὁ ιϲ· ἀφ' ἑαυτοῦ
σὺ τοῦτο λέγεις. ἢ ἄλλοι σοι εἶπον
περὶ ἐμοῦ· ἀπεκρίθη ὁ πιλᾶτος·
μήτι ἐγὼ ἰουδαῖός εἰμι; τὸ ἔθνος
τὸ σὸν καὶ οἱ ἀρχιερεῖς παρέδωκάν σε ἐμοί· τί ἐποίησας· ἀπεκρίθη ιϲ· ἡ βασιλεία ἡ ἐμὴ οὐκ ἔ-
ϲτιν ἐκ τοῦ κόσμου τούτου· εἰ

50. Codex 70 again: page 380.

Plate 51   99

7 0

ΚΑΤΑ ΙΩΑΝΝΗΝ 18 (31-36)

ὑμῶν κρίνατε αὐτόν . εἶπον οὖν

αὐτῷ οἱ 'Ιουδαῖοι , 'Ημῖν οὐκ ἔξεστιν

ἀποκτεῖναι οὐδένα , ἵνα ὁ λόγος

τοῦ 'Ι(ησο)ῦ πληρωθῇ ὅν εἶπεν σημαί-

-νων ποίῳ θανάτῳ·ἤμελλεν ἀπο-

-θνῄσκειν . Εἰσῆλθεν οὖν εἰς το

πραιτώριον πάλιν ὁ Πιλᾶτος καὶ

ἐφώνησεν τον 'Ι(ησου)ν καὶ εἶπεν αὐτῷ ,

Συ εἶ ὁ βασιλευς τῶν 'Ιουδαίων ;

'Απεκρίθη αὐτῷ ὁ 'Ι(ησοῦ)ς ,ἀφ'ἑαυτοῦ

συ τοῦτο λέγεις , ἤ ἄλλοι σοι εἶπον

περι ἐμοῦ ; ἀπεκτίθη ὁ Πιλᾶτος ,

Μήτι ἐγω 'Ιουδαῖός εἰμι . το ἔθνος

το σον καὶ οἱ ἀρχιερεῖς παρέδω-

-κάν σε ἐμοι . Τί ἐποίησας ; ἀπε-

-κρίθη 'Ι(ησοῦ)ς ,ἡ βασιλεία ἡ ἐμη οὐκ ἔ-

-στιν ἐκ τοῦ κόσμου τούτου . Εἰ

51. Transcription: John 18:31-36. The codex is a fine example of the
    "middle minuscule" of the *codices vetusti*.

52. Greek ms 89 of Paris, page 153. A less perfect and regular minuscule.

Plate 53   101

8 9 .

φάγωσιν το πάσχα . ἐξῆλθεν οὖν ὁ Πιλᾶ-

-τος πρὸς αὐτούς καὶ εἶπε, Τίνα κατηγορίαν

φέρετε κατα τοῦ ἀν(θρώπ)ου τούτου ; ἀπεκρίθησαν καὶ

εἶπον αὐτῷ ,Εἰ μὴ ἦν οὖτος κακοποιός ,οὐ-

-κ ἄν σοι παρεδώκαμεν αὐτόν . εἶπεν οὖν αὐτοῖς

ὁ Πιλᾶτος , Λάβετε αὐτον ὑμεῖς , καὶ κατα τον

νόμον ὑμῶν κρίνατε αὐτον . εἶπον δε αὐτῷ

οἱ 'Ιουδαῖοι , Ἡμῖν οὐκ ἔξεστιν ἀποκτεῖναι οὐδένα.

ἵνα ὁ λόγος τοῦ 'Ι(ησο)ῦ πληρωθῇ ὅν εἶπεν σημαί-

-νων, ποίῳ θανάτῳ ἔμελλεν ἀποθνήσκειν .

Εἰσῆλθεν οὖν πάλιν εἰς το πραιτώριον ὁ Πιλᾶ-

-τος καὶ ἐφώνησεν τον 'Ι(ησοῦ)ν καὶ εἶπεν αὐτῷ , Σὺ

εἶ ὁ βασιλευς τῶν 'Ιουδαίων ; ἀπεκρίνα-

-το ὁ 'Ι(ησοῦ)ς , 'Αφ'ἑαυτοῦ συ τοῦτο λέγεις ἤ ἄλλοι

σοι εἶπον περι ἐμοῦ ; ἀπεκρίθη ὁ Πιλᾶτος , Μή-

-τι ἐγω 'Ιουδαῖος εἰμι ; το ἔθνος το σον καὶ οἱ ἀρχι-

-ερεῖς παρέδωκαν σε ἐμοί . Τί ἐποίησας ;

ἀπεκρίθη 'Ι(ησοῦ)ς, ἡ βασιλεία ἡ ἐμη οὐκ ἔστιν ἐκ τοῦ

κόσμου τούτου . εἰ ἐκ τοῦ κόσμου τούτου ἦν ἡ βα-

-σιλεία ἡ ἐμή , οἱ ὑπηρέται ἄν οἱ ἐμοι ἠγωνίζον-

-το ,ἵνα μη παραδοθῶ τοῖς 'Ιουδαίοις . νῦν

δε ἡ βασιλεία ἡ ἐμη οὐκ ἔστιν ἐντεῦθεν . εἶπεν

οὖν αὐτῷ ὁ Πιλᾶτος , Οὐκοῦν βασιλευς εἶ σύ;

ἀπεκρίθη ὁ 'Ι(ησοῦ)ς , Συ λέγεις ὅτι βασιλεύς εἰμι.

ἐγω εἰς τοῦτο γεγέννημαι καὶ εἰς τοῦτο ἐλήλυθα εἰς

τον κόσμον , ἵνα μαρτυρήσω τῇ ἀληθείᾳ .

πᾶς ὁ ὤν ἐκ τῆς ἀληθείας ἀκούει μου τῆς

φωνῆς . λέγει αὐτῷ ὁ Πιλᾶτος , Τί ἐστιν ἀλή-

-θεια ; καὶ τοῦτο εἰπων πάλιν ἐξῆλθεν πρὸς τους 'Ιου-

(δαίους .)

53. A transcription that will enable to follow the ms text without
difficulty despite the numerous ligatures used in the twelfth century.

54. Greek ms 74 of Paris, page 204 verso, painting of Jesus before Pilate.

7 4

18   (32-34)

(ἥ)μελλεν ἀποθνήσκειν

Εἰσῆλθεν οὖν εἰς το πραιτώριον πάλιν ὁ Πιλᾶτος

και ἐφώνησεν τον 'Ι(ησοῦ)ν και εἶπεν αὐτῷ ,Συ εἶ ὁ βασι-

-λευς τῶν 'Ιουδαίων ;ἀπεκρίθη αὐτῷ ὁ 'Ι(ησοῦ)ς ἀφ'ἑ-

-αυτοῦ συ τοῦτο λέγεις ,ἥ ἄλλοι σοι εἶπον περι ἐμοῦ

55. Transcription: John 18:32-34.

56. Greek ms 74 again, page 204 recto, with text corresponding to the verso of Rylands Papyrus 457.

Plate 57　　　　　　　　　　　　　　105

· 7　4

1 8　　(37–39)

ὅτι βασιλεύς εἰμι ἐγώ . ἐγω εἰς τοῦτο γεγέννημαι
Και εἰς τοῦτο ἐλήλυθα εἰς τον κόσμον ἵνα μαρτυ-
-ρήσω τῇ ἀληθείᾳ. πᾶς ὁ ὤν ἐκ τῆς ἀληθείας
ἀκούει μου τῆς φωνῆς . λέγει αὐτῷ ὁ Πιλᾶτος
Τί ἐστιν ἀλήθεια ; και τοῦτο εἰπων πάλιν ἐξῆλθεν προς τους Ἰουδαίους .
και λέγει αὐτοῖς ,ἐγω οὐ-
-δεμίαν αἰτίαν εὑρίσκω
ἐν αὐτῷ . ἔστι　δε συνή-
Θεια ὑμῖν ἵνα ἕνα ὑμῖν
ἀπολύσω ἐν τῷ πάσχα .
βούλεσθε οὖν ὑμῖν ἀπο-
-λύσω τον βασιλέα τῶν Ἰουδαίων ; ἐκραύγα-
Σαν οὖν πάλιν λέγοντες , μη τοῦτον , ἀλλα τον
βαραββᾶν .ἦν δε ὁ βαραββᾶς λῃστής .

57. Transcription, showing how a majuscule letter projects into the margin at the beginning of every fourth line.

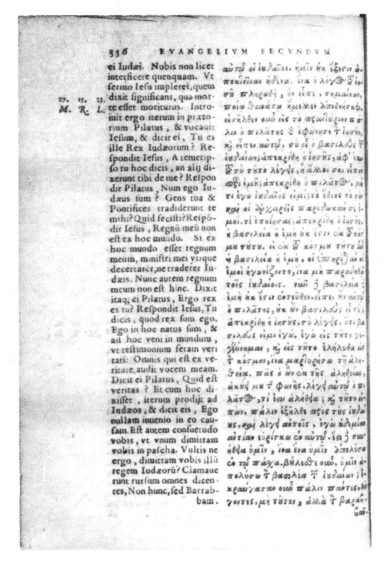

58. Page 336 of Erasmus' Greek-Latin edition.

Plate 59 107

ΕΚΔΟΣΙΣ ΕΡΑΣΜΟΥ

Αὐτῷ οἱ 'Ιουδαῖοι . 'Ημῖν οὐκ ἔξεστιν ἀ-
-ποκτεῖναι οὐδένα . ἵνα ὁ λόγος τοῦ 'Ιη-
-σοῦ πληρωθῇ ,ὃν εἶπε σημαίνων
ποίῳ θανάτῳ ἤμελλεν ἀποθνήσκειν .
εἰσῆλθεν οὖν εἰς το πραιτώριον πά-
-λιν ὁ Πιλᾶτος καὶ ἐφώνησε τον 'Ιησοῦν
καὶ εἶπεν αὐτῷ ,Συ εἶ ὁ βασιλευς τῶν
'Ιουδαίων ; ἀπεκρίθη ὁ 'Ιησοῦς , 'Αφ' ἑαυ-
-τοῦ συ τοῦτο λέγεις ἢ ἄλλοι σοι εἶπον
περι ἐμοῦ ; ἀπεκρίθη ὁ Πιλᾶτος Μή-
-τι ἐγω 'Ιουδαῖος εἰμι ; το ἔθνος το σον
καὶ οἱ ἀρχιερεῖς παρέδωκάν ἐ-
-μοι , Τί ἐποίησας ; ἀπεκρίθη ὁ 'Ιησοῦς
'Η βασιλεία ἡ ἐμη οὐκ ἔστιν ἐκ τοῦ κόσ-
-μου τούτου . εἰ ἐκ τοῦ κόσμου τούτου ἦν
ἡ βασιλεία ἡ ἐμη , οἱ ὑπηρέται οἱ -
ἐμοι ἠγωνίζοντο , ἵνα μη παραδοθῶ
τοῖς 'Ιουδαίοις . νῦν δε ἡ βασιλεία ἡ
ἐμη οὐκ ἔστιν ἐντεῦθεν . εἶπεν οὖν αὐτῷ
ὁ Πιλᾶτος ,Οὐκ οὖν βασιλευς εἶ σύ ;
ἀπεκρίθη ὁ 'Ιησοῦς , Συ λέγεις ὅτι βα-
-σιλευς εἰμι ἐγω . 'Εγω εἰς τοῦτο γε-
-γέννημαι καὶ εἰς τοῦτο ἐλήλυθα εἰς
τον κόσμον , ἵνα μαρτυρήσω τῇ ἀλη-
-θεία . πᾶς ὁ ὢν ἐκ τῆς ἀληθείας
ἀκούει μου τῆς φωνῆς . λέγει αὐτῷ ὁ Πι-
-λᾶτος , Τί ἐστιν ἀλήθεια ; καὶ τοῦτο εἰ-
-πων πάλιν ἐξῆλθεν προς τους 'Ιουδαί-
-ους , καὶ λέγει αὐτοῖς , 'Εγω οὐδεμίαν
αἰτίαν εὑρίσκω ἐν αὐτῷ .ἔστιν δε συν-
-ήθεια ὑμῖν , ἵνα ἕνα ὑμῖν ἀπολύσω
ἐν τῷ πάσχα . βούλεσθε οὖν ὑμῖν ἀ-
-πολύσω τον βασιλέα τῶν 'Ιουδαίων ; ἐ-
-κραύγασαν οὖν πάλιν πάντες , λε-
-γοντες , μη τοῦτον ἀλλα τόν βαραββᾶν.

59. Transcription of the Greek text in modern Greek type, enabling
the reader to follow the older Greek type quite readily. The older
type reproduced the writing used in fourteenth and fifteenth
century manuscripts. The writing of late minuscule as found in
the *codices recentiores* was imitated in printing down to the
seventeenth century.

Ἰωάννϲ.   Caρ.vi

'εμ, Ἰω'ορεματι Ἰω "ιλιω." εκείμον "λήψεϲ
θε."ωϲ' Δύνασθε' υμείϲ' ωιστεύσαι' Δόξαν
"ωαρά'αλλήλων'λαμξανοντεϲ."και Ἱηρ'λο-
ξαν Ἱηρ'ωαρά Ἰον'μοριον' θεού' ου'ζητειτε.
' μη ' Δοκειτε' οτι 'εγω ' κατηγορήσω' υμων
"προϲ Ἰον'πατερα."εστιν ο'κατηγορων'υμων
'μωσήϲ'ειϲ'ον'υμειϲ'ηλπικατε.'ει'γαρ'επι
στευετε' μωσει.'επιστευετε'αν'εμοι."ωερι'γαρ
"εμον'εκεινοϲ'εγραψεν." ει'Δε' Τοιϲ'εκεινον
"γραμμασιν' ου' ωιστευετε'ωωϲ;Τοιϲ'εμοιϲ
'ρημασι'ωιστεύσετε.   Caρ.ϛ.

Latin column:

'in'nomine' suo'illum' accipietis. ооо
Quid'vos'potestis'credere qui'gloriam
'ab'invicem'accipitis:'i'gloriam que co
'a'solo'deo est'non'queritis. ссссссо
Nolite'putare'q'ego'accusaturus'sim
'apud'patre. Est'qui'accusat'vos L'vos
'mosico'i'quo'vos'sperans. Si'eni'cre
deretis'mosi'crederetis'forsitan'mihi. De
'me'enim'ille'scripsit. Si'autem'illius
'litteris'non'creditis:'quo'verbis'meis
'credetis?   Caρ.ϛ.

60. Fourth Gospel, chapter 6, in the Alcalá Polyglot of 1514–1517.

Plate 61   109

274   XVIII, 32   ΚΑΤΑ ΙΩΑΝΝΗΝ

ἀποκτεῖναι οὐδένα. ³²ἵνα ὁ λόγοσ τοῦ ἰησοῦ πληρωθῇ, σημαίνων ποίῳ θανάτῳ ἤμελλεν ἀποθνήσκειν. ³³εἰσῆλθεν οὖν εἰσ τὸ
πραιτώριον πάλιν ὁ πιλᾶτοσ, καὶ ἐφώνησεν τὸν ἰησοῦν καὶ εἶπεν αὐτῷ· σὺ εἶ ὁ βασιλεὺσ τῶν ἰουδαίων; ³⁴ἀπεκρίθη αὐτῷ ὁ
ἰησοῦσ· ἀπὸ σεαυτοῦ τοῦτο εἶπασ, ἢ ἄλλοι σοι εἶπον περὶ ἐμοῦ;
³⁵ἀπεκρίθη ὁ πιλᾶτοσ· μὴ ἐγὼ ἰουδαῖόσ εἰμι; τὸ ἔθνοσ τὸ σὸν
καὶ ὁ ἀρχιερεὺσ παρέδωκάν σε ἐμοί· τί ἐποίησασ; ³⁶ἀπεκρίθη
ἰησοῦσ· ἡ ἐμὴ βασιλεία οὐκ ἔστιν ἐκ τοῦ κόσμου τούτου· εἰ
ἐκ τοῦ κόσμου τούτου ἦν ἡ ἐμὴ βασιλεία, καὶ οἱ ὑπηρέται οἱ
ἐμοὶ ἠγωνίζοντο ἂν ἵνα μὴ παραδοθῶ τοῖσ ἰουδαίοισ· νῦν δὲ ἡ
ἐμὴ βασιλεία οὐκ ἔστιν ἐντεῦθεν. ³⁷εἶπεν οὖν αὐτῷ ὁ πιλᾶτοσ·
οὐκοῦν βασιλεὺσ εἶ σύ; ἀπεκρίθη ὁ ἰησοῦσ· σὺ λέγεισ, ὅτι βασιλεύσ εἰμι· ἐγὼ εἰσ τοῦτο γεγέννημαι καὶ εἰσ τοῦτο ἐλήλυθα
εἰσ τὸν κόσμον, ἵνα μαρτυρήσω περὶ τῆσ ἀληθείασ· πᾶσ ὁ ὢν
τῆσ ἀληθείασ ἀκούει μου τῆσ φωνῆσ. ³⁸λέγει αὐτῷ ὁ πιλᾶτοσ·
τίσ ἐστιν ἀλήθεια; καὶ τοῦτο εἰπὼν πάλιν ἐξῆλθεν πρὸσ τοὺσ
ἰουδαίουσ καὶ λέγει αὐτοῖσ· ἐγὼ οὐδεμίαν αἰτίαν εὑρίσκω ἐν
αὐτῷ. ³⁹ἔστιν δὲ συνήθεια ὑμῖν ἵνα ἕνα ἀπολύσω ὑμῖν ἐν τῷ
πάσχα· βούλεσθε οὖν ἵνα ἀπολύσω ὑμῖν τὸν βασιλέα τῶν ἰουδαίων; ⁴⁰ἐκραύγασαν οὖν πάλιν λέγοντεσ· μὴ τοῦτον, ἀλλὰ
τὸν βαραββᾶν. ἦν δὲ ὁ βαραββᾶσ λῃστήσ.

XIX.

¹Τότε οὖν λαβὼν ὁ πιλᾶτοσ τὸν ἰησοῦν ἐμαστίγωσεν. ²καὶ
οἱ στρατιῶται πλέξαντεσ στέφανον ἐξ ἀκανθῶν ἐπέθηκαν αὐ-

32 πληρωθη: ᶜadd ον ειπεν   34 ᶜσυ τουτο λεγεισ   35 ᶜμητι εγω | ᶜοι αρ-
χιερεισ   37 μαρτυρησω ᵃ(ipse ᶜ corr?: ᵇ-ση | περι τ. αλ.: ᶜτη αληθεια | ᶜεκ
τησ αληθ.   38 τισ: ᶜτι

32 πληρωθη: add ον ειπεν   33 παλιν εισ τ. πραιτ. ο πειλατ.   34 om αυτω ο
α. σ. συ τουτ. λεγεισ | ειπον σοι   35 πειλατ. | μητι εγω | οι αρχιερεισ   36 η βα-
σιλ. η εμη | 1, η βασ. η εμη, om και | αυ: suppl est | νυν δε η βασ. η εμη   37 πει-
λατ. | ο ων εκ τησ   38 πειλατ. | τισ: τι | ευρισκ. εν αυ. αιτ.   39 om εν | om ινα
sec   XIX, 1 ελαβεν ο πειλατ. τ. ιησ. και

32 πληρωθη: add ον ειπε   34 αφ εαυτου συ του. λεγεισ   35 μητι εγω | οι αρ-
χιερεισ   36 ο ιησουσ | η βασιλ. η εμη ter | om και | αν post υπηρεται   37 ειμι
εγω· εγω εισ | τη αληθεια | εκ τησ αληθ.   38 τισ: τι   39 υμιν απολυσω bis | om
ινα sec   40 παλιν: add παντεσ   XIX, 1 ελαβεν et και εμαστιγ.

*934 18, 35. ΚΑΤΑ ΙΩΑΝΝΗΝ

σοι εἶπον περὶ ἐμοῦ; 35 ἀπεκρίθη ὁ Πειλᾶτοσ· μήτι ἐγὼ Ἰουδαῖόσ
εἰμι; τὸ ἔθνοσ τὸ σὸν καὶ οἱ ἀρχιερεῖσ παρέδωκάν σε ἐμοί· τί
ἐποίησασ; 36 ἀπεκρίθη Ἰησοῦσ· ἡ βασιλεία ἡ ἐμὴ οὐκ ἔστιν ἐκ
τοῦ κόσμου τούτου. εἰ ἐκ τοῦ κόσμου τούτου ἦν ἡ βασιλεία ἡ ἐμή,
οἱ ὑπηρέται ἂν οἱ ἐμοὶ ἠγωνίζοντο, ἵνα μὴ παραδοθῶ τοῖσ Ἰου-
δαίοισ· νῦν δὲ ἡ βασιλεία ἡ ἐμὴ οὐκ ἔστιν ἐντεῦθεν. 37 [180.1]
εἶπεν οὖν αὐτῷ ὁ Πειλᾶτοσ· οὐκοῦν βασιλεὺσ εἶ σύ; ἀπεκρίθη
ὁ Ἰησοῦσ· σὺ λέγεισ, ὅτι βασιλεύσ εἰμι. [181.10] ἐγὼ εἰσ τοῦτο γεγέν-
8, 47 νημαι καὶ εἰσ τοῦτο ἐλήλυθα εἰσ τὸν κόσμον, ἵνα μαρτυρήσω τῇ
ἀληθείᾳ· πᾶσ ὁ ὢν ἐκ τῆσ ἀληθείασ ἀκούει μου τῆσ φωνῆσ.
38 λέγει αὐτῷ ὁ Πειλᾶτοσ· τί ἐστιν ἀλήθεια; καὶ τοῦτο εἰπὼν
19, 4 πάλιν ἐξῆλθεν πρὸσ τοὺσ Ἰουδαίουσ, [182.9] καὶ λέγει αὐτοῖσ· ἐγὼ

35. πειλατ. cum AB*D[supp] ... ς Ln Ti πιλ. cum ℵB[3]LY unc rell al omn. vid | μητι (et. Or[4,401] et ℵ[c]): ℵ* 1. 2[pe] 6[pe] μη | οι (D[supp] om) αρχιερεισ (et. ℵ[c] Or): ℵ* b e ο αρχιερευσ | εμοι: A μοι

36. ῑς̄ cum ℵABCD[supp]LXYΓΛΠ*et[3] unc[7] al plu Cyr[4,1038] ... ς (Gb[oo]) praem ο cum ΛΠ[2] al mu | η βασιλ. η εμη pri: ℵ η εμη βασιλ. | Y a τουτου pri ad τουτου alterum transilit | η βασ. η εμη sec (et. Or[1,375. 3,230. 562] et [4,23]): ℵD[supp] 73. 106. 124. Chr[mosc1] η εμη βασ. | οι υπηρεται: ℵ praem και | αν post οι υπηρετ. cum AD[supp]YΓΔΛΠ unc[7] al pler q Or [3,562] Hier[ecclesiast] (accuratissime q Hier *ministri utique mei*), item *ministri mei utique* c f ff[2] g vg[cle] et[cdd] (sed non am for fu al) aeth ... ℵH[mg supp]LX 1. 33. 69. 91. 124. 249. 299. arm Or[1,375] et [3,230] et [4,23] Chr[8,565] Cyr[4,1038] post ηγωνιζοντο (Chr -σαντο) pon ... B* om, nec exprim a b e am for fu, nec magis vv. aliae | παραδοθω: D[supp] 69. παραδω | η βασ. η εμη tertio loc: ℵ η εμη βασ.

37. πειλατοσ cum AB*D[supp] (sed cf alibi, ubi passim ℵCDIRT accedunt) ... ς Ln Ti πιλ. cum ℵB[3] rell omn[vid] | απεκριθη: U aeth praem και ... K syr[sch] sah cop[ds] Cyr[4,1039] add αυτω | ο ῑς̄ cum ℵABD[supp]YΛΠ unc[7] al plu Cyr[4,1039] ... Ti om ο cum LXΓΔ 28. 33. 262. al[50] | εγω semel cum ℵBD[supp]LY 1. 18. 33. 69. 124. 235. 249. 6[pe] al pauc a c fos arm Chr[8,565] Cyr Cyp[297] Amb[ioseph 12], item e aeth qui neutrum εγω habent ... ς Ti εγω. εγω, Ln εγω. [εγω], cum AXΓΔΛΠ unc[7] al pler b f ff[2] g q vg sah cop syr[utr] et[hr] go | γεγεννημαι (Γ 69. al[10] ac plures γεγενημαι): A praem και | τη αληθεια (ℵ[c]): ℵ* περι τησ αληθειασ. Cf e *testimonium dicam veritatis*; it[rell] vg *testimonium perhibeam (reddam q) veritati.* | εκ τησ αληθειασ (et. ℵ[c]): ℵ* om εκ

38. πειλατοσ cum AB*D[supp] ... ς Ln Ti πιλ. ut v. 37 | τι (ℵ[c]): ℵ* τισ | αληθεια: 1. al aliq η αληθ. | ουδεμ. ευρισκ. εν αυτ. αιτιαν cum BLX 249. (299. εν αυτ. αιτ. ουδεμ. ευρ.) b c e ff[2] g vg aeth (a *nullam in illo invenio causam*; f Quaest[65,2880] *nullam invenio causam in eo*) Cyr [4,1040] ... ς ουδεμ. αιτ. ευρ. εν αυτ. cum ℵΑΓΔΛΠ unc[7] al pler q go syr[utr] et[hr] arm Chr[8,568]. Similiter sah cop *non invenio ullam causam in eo*

62. The great eighth edition of Tischendorf, showing the notes on only a few verses.

Plate 63   111

18, 24–36   Κατα Ιωαννην   287

24 ¹ἀπέστειλεν οὖν αὐτὸν ὁ Ἄννας δεδεμένον πρὸς 65

18. 25 Καϊαφᾶν τὸν ἀρχιερέα.² Ἦν δὲ Σίμων Πέτρος 174,1
ἑστὼς καὶ θερμαινόμενος. εἶπον οὖν αὐτῷ· μὴ 175,1
καὶ σὺ ἐκ τῶν μαθητῶν αὐτοῦ εἶ; ἠρνήσατο ἐκεῖνος

26 καὶ εἶπεν· οὐκ εἰμί. λέγει εἷς ἐκ τῶν δούλων
τοῦ ἀρχιερέως, συγγενὴς ὢν οὗ ἀπέκοψεν Πέτρος
τὸ ὠτίον· οὐκ ἐγώ σε εἶδον ἐν τῷ κήπῳ μετ'

18,38. 27 αὐτοῦ; πάλιν οὖν ἠρνήσατο^TΠέτρος, καὶ εὐθέως
ἀλέκτωρ ἐφώνησεν.

23—19,15 :
Mt 27,2.11—30. 28   Ἄγουσιν οὖν τὸν Ἰησοῦν ἀπὸ τοῦ Καϊαφᾶ εἰς 66
Mc 15,1—19.
L 23,1—25.   τὸ πραιτώριον· ἦν δὲ πρωΐ·* καὶ αὐτοὶ οὐκ εἰσῆλ- 176,1
θον εἰς τὸ πραιτώριον, ἵνα μὴ μιανθῶσιν ἀλλὰ 177,10

29 φάγωσιν τὸ πάσχα. ἐξῆλθεν οὖν ὁ Πιλᾶτος ἔξω
πρὸς αὐτοὺς καὶ φησίν· τίνα κατηγορίαν φέρετε

30 ^Tτοῦ ἀνθρώπου τούτου; ἀπεκρίθησαν καὶ εἶπαν
αὐτῷ· εἰ μὴ ἦν οὗτος ʿκακὸν ποιῶνˋ, οὐκ ἂν σοι

19,6 s. 31 παρεδώκαμεν αὐτόν. εἶπεν οὖν αὐτοῖς °ὁ Πιλᾶτος·
Act 18,15.   λάβετε ^Tαὐτὸν ὑμεῖς, καὶ κατὰ τὸν νόμον ὑμῶν
κρίνατε °²αὐτόν. εἶπον^Tαὐτῷ οἱ Ἰουδαῖοι· ἡμῖν

32 οὐκ ἔξεστιν ἀποκτεῖναι οὐδένα· ἵνα ὁ λόγος τοῦ
3,14 I Mt 20,19p.   Ἰησοῦ πληρωθῇ ὃν εἶπεν σημαίνων ποίῳ θανάτῳ

33 ἤμελλεν ἀποθνήσκειν. Εἰσῆλθεν οὖν ͠πάλιν εἰς 67
τὸ πραιτώριον² ὁ Πιλᾶτος καὶ ἐφώνησεν τὸν 178,1

12,13 I Ἰησοῦν καὶ εἶπεν αὐτῷ· σὺ εἶ ὁ βασιλεὺς τῶν
Mt 16,13 p. **34** Ἰουδαίων; ¹ ἀπεκρίθη ^TἸησοῦς· ʿἀφ' ἑαυτοῦˋ °σὺ 179,10

1,11. 35 τοῦτο λέγεις, ἢ ἄλλοι ͠εἶπόν σοι² περὶ ἐμοῦ; ἀπεκρίθη ὁ Πιλᾶτος· ʿμήτι ἐγὼ Ἰουδαῖός εἰμι; τὸ
ἔθνος τὸ σὸν καὶ ʿοἱ ἀρχιερεῖςˋᶠπαρέδωκάν σε ἐμοί·

3,3.5. 36 τί ἐποίησας; ¹ ἀπεκρίθη Ἰησοῦς· ἡ βασιλεία ἡ ἐμὴ
8,23.
L 17,20 s; 19,12.   οὐκ ἔστιν ἐκ τοῦ κόσμου τούτου· εἰ ἐκ τοῦ κόσμου
Mt 4,8; 26,53.   τούτου ἦν ἡ ʿβασιλεία ἡ ἐμήˋ, οἱ ὑπηρέται ͠ἂν οἱ ἐμοὶ

27 Το ΝΡΘαl; W : txt ϞEGpm   29 Τχατα P66 CRΘpl; S   30 ʿx. ποιησας
Ν*. : χαχοποιων U*pc : -οιος ΡΘpl; S : txt BLW   31 UBC*; H | ʿTουν P66. |
O² P66vid Ν* W 565 al c; T | ¹Τουν ΝΡαl; T : δε AΘ 565 pm : txt P66vid BCpc   33 ͠
2—41 ΚΡΘpm; T : txt P52.66 Ϟpe   34 Το ΚCRΘpm; S : txt P66vid Bal | ʿαπο
σεαυτου P66 ϞN; H : txt ΡWΘ 33 pl | O P66* Ν*pc lat Non | ͠ΚΡΘpm; T : txt P66
BC*pe   35 ʿμη Ν Wpc : [μη] γαρ P66. | ʿο-ευς Ν*δε αι F-χεν e.   36 ʿεμη
βασ. ΚΝΘpc; S | ᶠ2—41 Ϟαl; H : 2—4 P66vid B* : txt Ρpm

63. Page 287 in the 25th edition of Nestle (by Erwin Nestle and Kurt
Aland).

ΚΑΤΑ ΙΩΑΝΝΗΝ .   1   8   .(28–40)

28. Ἄγουσιν οὖν τον Ἰησοῦν ἀπο τοῦ Καϊάφα εἰς το
πραιτώριον . ἦν δε πρωΐ. και αὐτοὶ οὐκ εἰσῆλθον
εἰς το πραιτώριον , ἵνα μη μιανθῶσιν ἀλλα φάγωσιν
το πάσχα.

29. ἐξῆλθεν οὖν ὁ Πιλᾶτος ἔξω προς αὐτους και φησίν,
Τίνα κατηγορίαν φέρετε κατα τοῦ ἀνθρώπου τούτου ;

30. ἀπεκρίθησαν και εἶπαν αὐτῷ , Εἰ μη ἦν οὗτος
κακον ποιῶν , οὐκ ἄν σοι παρεδώκαμεν αὐτόν.

31. εἶπεν οὖν αὐτοῖς ὁ Πιλᾶτος , Λάβετε αὐτον ὑμεῖς
και κατα τον νόμον ὑμῶν κρίνατε αὐτον . εἶπον
οὖν αὐτῷ οἱ Ἰουδαῖοι , Ἡμῖν οὐκ ἔξεστιν
ἀποκτεῖναι οὐδενα .

32. ἵνα ὁ λόγος τοῦ Ἰησοῦ πληρωθῇ ὃν εἶπεν σημαίνων
ποίῳ θανάτῳ ἤμελλεν ἀποθνῄσκειν .

33.Εἰσῆλθεν οὖν πάλιν εἰς το πραιτώριον ὁ Πιλᾶτος
και ἐφώνησεν τον Ἰησοῦν και εἶπεν αὐτῷ ,
Συ εἶ ὁ βασιλευς τῶν Ἰουδαίων ;

34. ἀπεκρίθη Ἰησοῦς , Ἀπο σεαυτοῦ συ τοῦτο λέγεις
ἤ ἄλλοι εἶπον σοι περι ἐμοῦ ;

35. ἀπεκρίθη ὁ Πιλᾶτος, Μήτι ἐγω Ἰουδαῖός εἰμι ;
το ἔθνος το σον και οἱ ἀρχιερεῖς παρέδωκάν σε
ἐμοι . Τί ἐποίησας ;

36. ἀπεκρίθη Ἰησοῦς , Ἡ βασιλεία ἡ ἐμη οὐκ ἔστιν
ἐκ τοῦ κόσμου τούτου . εἰ ἐκ τοῦ κόσμου τούτου
ἦν ἡ βασιλεία ἡ ἐμη , οἱ ὑπηρέται οἱ ἐμοι ἠγωνι—
—ζοντο (ἄν) ἵνα μη παραδοθῶ τοῖς Ἰουδαίοις ,
νῦν δε ἡ βασιλεία ἡ ἐμη οὐκ ἔστιν ἐντεῦθεν.

37. εἶπεν οὖν αὐτῷ ὁ Πιλᾶτος , Οὐκοῦν βασιλευς εἶ
σύ ; ἀπεκρίθη ὁ Ἰησοῦς , Συ λέγεις ὅτι βασιλεύς
εἰμι . Ἐγω εἰς τοῦτο γεγέννημαι και εἰς τοῦτο
ἐλήλυθα εἰς τον κόσμον , ἵνα μαρτυρήσω τῇ ἀληθείᾳ.
πᾶς ὁ ὢν ἐκ τῆς ἀληθείας ἀκούει μου τῆς φωνῆς .

38. λέγει αὐτῷ ὁ Πιλᾶτος , Τί ἐστιν ἀλήθεια ;
και τοῦτο εἰπων πάλιν ἐξῆλθεν προς τους Ἰουδαίους ,
και λέγει αὐτοῖς , Ἐγω οὐδεμίαν εὑρίσκω ἐν αὐτῷ
αἰτίαν ;

39. ἔστιν δε συνήθεια ὑμῖν ἵνα ἕνα ἀπολύσω ὑμῖν ἐν τῷ
πάσχα . βούλεσθε οὖν ἀπολύσω ὑμῖν τον βασιλέα τῶν
Ἰουδαίων ;

40. ἐκραύγασαν οὖν πάλιν λέγοντες , Μη τοῦτον ἀλλα
τον βαραββᾶν . ἦν δε ὁ βαραββᾶς λῃστής .

64. The episode of Jesus before Pilate in *The Greek New Testament* edited by Aland, Black, Metzger, and Wikgren (1967).

Note: There is no grave accent in the Greek manuscripts; the omission facilitated copying. Since the Greek accent was musical (a raising of the voice), the grave accent meant really an absence of accent. Consequently the simplification of the accentual system by the copyists does not represent a real omission.